WHY GOD?:
The Existential Christian

Darrah Stedham-Angus

Dedicated to all those Christians out there who are still searching and hoping to find...

TABLE OF CONTENTS

FOREWORD

Upon picking up this book, your first question might be, "What is an Existential Christian?". The simple answer is, a Christian who endeavors to ask themselves, "Why am I a Christian?". At some point the answer of "because I want to go to heaven", must and needs to become more than just than our primary reason for being a Christian. These readings endeavor to answer not only that question, but the questions we might have all had as Christians and have been to afraid to ask, and even more afraid to answer. My hope is that as you read this book, you find the deeper meaning of what it is to be a Christian, and how this can help not only to improve your life, but the lives of others.

Once Upon A Time,
There Was A Girl and Her Father...

DEMONS OF DOUBT AND MUSTARD SEED FAITH

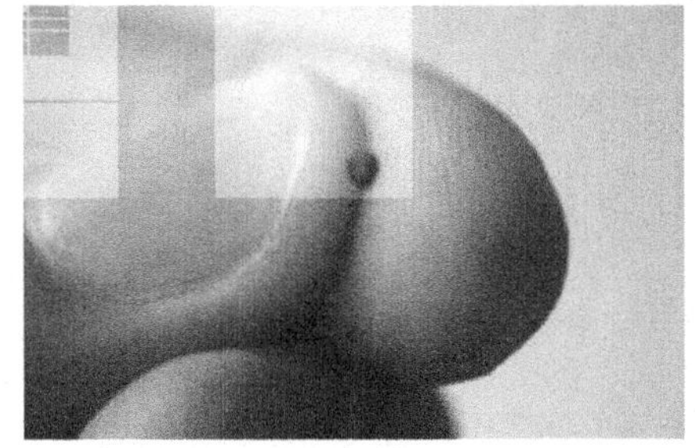

Once upon a time, in a land not far from yours,
there was a girl and her father:

"Father, how much Faith does it take to please God?" the girl asked. "Not much. All we need is Faith the size of a mustard seed, and God will do the rest." The father answered.

Webster defines doubt as*: to lack confidence in: distrust.* As Christians, most of us would deny distrusting God, as it fundamentally goes against every foundation of our Faith. But let's ask ourselves a few honest questions. Even though we claim to know and believe in the extent of God's power, do we ever doubt Him? When we are confronted with difficult situations, do we think it out instead of letting Faith in? Do we try to find ways to solve it, instead of having Faith in God to either show us how to work it out, or allow Him to work it out without us even having to try?

At times it can seem difficult to believe that God will work out our *immediate* situations. As Christians we all carry the general belief and Faith in God's ability to work "it" (problems, situations, dilemmas, issues, etcetera) out. But do we ever put this Faith into practice, or do we put began to doubt (distrust) God's power?

In Matthew 17, there is a story about a boy that was possessed by a demon. In the story, the disciples tried (unsuccessfully) to remove the demon from the boy. Jesus became upset at the disciples for their inability to heal the demon-possessed boy and in the end, Jesus approached the boy, rebuked the demon, and the demon left the boy's body. Sometime later (and in private) the disciples asked Jesus why they were unable to remove the demon from the boy, and this is what Jesus answered:

Matthew 17:20

New Living Translation (NLT)

20 "You don't have enough faith," Jesus told them. "I tell you the truth, if you had faith even as small as a mustard seed, you could say to this mountain, 'Move from here to there,' and it would move. **Nothing would be impossible.**

What demons do you have, that you have
not been able to cast out?

In this scripture it seems as if Jesus is speaking directly to us instead of his disciples. Sometimes I have wondered, why a mustard seed? Logic tells us that in order to move mountains, we would need mountain-sized faith. But the bible tells us that Faith the size of a mustard seed is all it takes.

Looking at the picture above, it would seem evident to us all that everyone has at least that much Faith, right? But according to the scripture, many of us lack mustard-seed sized Faith. How many times have we begged and pleaded with our mountains to move, and they have remained right where they are?

Doesn't faith the size of a mustard seed seem easy enough to muster? For a child, it is nothing to conjure a mustard seeds' worth of Faith and more. But for us adults, life experience has taught us to rely on our eyes and our brains, more than the words of Jesus Christ. Sometimes for us, finding a mustard seed's worth of Faith within our hearts requires a super-human ability. When and why did we start to allow demons of doubt to creep within our souls? Where has our Faith gone?

I must admit, that at numerous times in my life it has been difficult to rely solely on God for help. I feel that I am smart, capable and can solve my own problems. I believe that many of us are not trying to be faithless, but instead are trying to take responsibility for or own behaviors and choices, and the outcomes of these acts. While this may seem right in man's eyes to fix it all on our own, it is not so in God's. He wants us to rely on him.

If a mustard seed of Faith is all it takes to move mountains, then let's find our spiritual mustard seeds, and start moving these mountains of doubt, distrust, pain and fear out of our lives. Can you imagine a life without these? Now _That_ is a life of true freedom, peace, and clarity. Imagine walking in that every day. Imagine walking in Faith every day. How would that feel to us if we could only find that mustard seed

ENTITLEMENT AND EXPECTATION

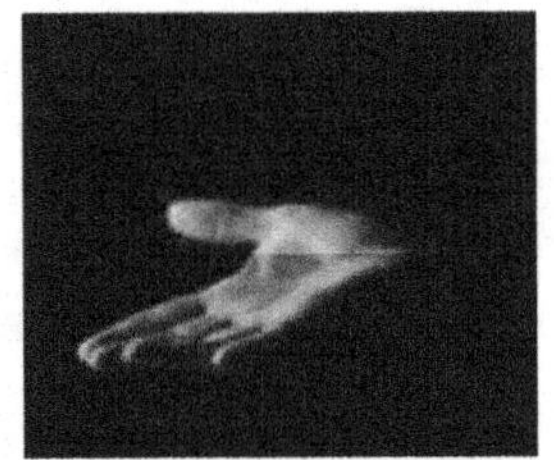

Once upon a time, in a land not far from yours,
there was a girl and her father:

"Father, I've been a good girl and I've been praying for a puppy. Why hasn't God answered my prayer?" the girl asked. "Why do you think He should?" the father asked in return. "Because I deserve it! I've been a good girl!" The girl answered emphatically. "God doesn't give to you because you deserve it. God gives to you because He loves you." the father said. "Then why should I be a good girl if I'm not going to get anything for it?" the girl asked. "The point of being a good girl is not to get something in return, it is to show God that you love him too." The father answered.

Have you ever been told that good things happen to good people? Or, that if you do good and follow all the religious rules and edicts, that your every desire will be your reward from God? Haven't we all been told this in some form at one time or another in our walk as Christians? In the back of our heads do we do good deeds *Expecting* great rewards? Do we live our lives with God and walk with Him feeling *Entitled* to the best of the world around us? Are we disappointed and hurt when things don't go our way, but instead goes well for someone who is not a believer?

At what point in our walk with God did we start to feel *Entitled* to everything around us? At what point did we start to expect God to do things for us, based <u>solely</u> on "good behavior"?

What we must understand is, God owes us nothing. Yes, this is a crazy notion, but God *owes* us nothing. Nothing about us as humans deserves God's pleasure. Everything that God gives to us, is given to us by Grace. And yes, I'm sure we've all heard Grace used in a thousand different ways, but let's just look at Grace as is. The dictionary defines Grace as "<u>*unmerited* divine</u>

assistance". This simply means, that you get something good, which you are not worthy of. This is what Grace really is. It's not love or forgiveness. Each one of these words has its own stand-alone definition, and we in the Christian Faith try to meld them together when they are indeed separate. We need to stop running around mad at God and the world, because we are not getting what we want as if we were *Entitled* to it <u>solely</u> through our "superior" behavior. It doesn't work like that.

Whatever good things God has put into your life, are not there because you deserve them, *Expect* them, or are *Entitled* to them. The good things you have, are given to you by God's Grace. These good things (blessings), are your undeserved rewards given to you by Grace because God loves you. This is what makes our Faith so great, and I feel is a main source of inspiration for wanting to live right and do good. We don't live Faithfully because we *Expect* from God. We live Faithfully because of all the good things that God has given us (i.e. life, health, strength, family, etc.) that we didn't deserve in the first place. <u>Holy Christian Living</u> is our way of showing God gratitude and saying thanks.

The message which I'm trying to convey is: We
don't live to get, we live to thank!

1 Corinthians 15:10

New International Version (NIV)

[10]*But by the grace of God I am what I am…*

Ephesians 2:8-10

New Living Translation (NLT)

[8]*God saved you by his grace when you believed. And you can't take credit for this; it is a gift from God.* [9]*Salvation is not a reward for the good things we have done, so none of us can boast about it.* [10]*For we are God's masterpiece. He has created us anew in Christ*

Jesus, so we can do the good things he planned for us long ago.

IS CHOICE A GIFT OR A CURSE?

Once upon a time in a land not far from yours,
there was a girl and her father:

"Daughter, do you know one of the greatest gifts that
God has given to man?" the father asked. "No father,
what is it?" the girl asked in return. "Choice." The father
answered. "Is it really, father?" the girl asked in return.

Each and every one of us has the capacity to be either:
light or dark, good or evil, selfless or selfish, Christian or
satanic, and so on. And, on any given day, if we didn't try
to control every urge that we have, we would constantly
fluctuate from one to the other. Why is this? Wouldn't
it be easier just to be one _or_ the other? Completely good
or completely bad? Wouldn't this be true peace?

In the bible it says that we are endowed
with a gift, the gift of choice.

1 Corinthians 8:9
Amplified Bible (AMP)

*9 Only be careful that this power of choice (this permission
and liberty to do as you please) which is yours, does not
[somehow] become a hindrance (cause of stumbling) to the
weak or overscrupulous [giving them an impulse to sin].*

If we were only programed to be one way or the other
(good or bad), we wouldn't have this "gift" of choice.
Sometimes I wonder if having choices is good or not?
Wouldn't it just be easier, not to have to choose?

Have you ever asked yourself, "What if we (as mankind) only had
the capacity of doing good, and never knew what it was to do or
be evil?" After asking myself this same question, another one
came to mind: Is choice really man's gift or is it man's curse?

At one time (according to the story of creation), Adam and

Eve only had the capacity to be good. All their actions and thoughts were pure. It wasn't until they ate of the fruit of the tree *"in the midst of the garden"* that they were given this "gift" of choice between deciding to do good or evil, which now returns us to the question: Is choice a gift or a curse?

Sometimes in my ideal Christian mind, I truly wish that none of us had ever known what it is to be evil. I wish that we never knew what it was to feel selfishness, and pain, and the mindless actions that result from a mind and heart overwhelmed with grief and sadness.

Maybe this is what makes choice so powerful? The fact that we can choose to take the easy way out in our lifetime of situations. But, when we use choice to go against our selfish impulses and do what is right, what is good and what is Holy…how can God not get the Glory?

I once heard a preacher say that *"A transformed life is the most powerful testimony"*. A person who makes the choice to give their life to God, when not forced to, is what makes choice a gift. When we choose right, when we do right, when we live holy and when we help others to make that right choice, *proves* that choice is a gift.

When we use choice to selfishly chase after our own ambitions, and neglect the needs and wants of others, is when choice becomes a curse. In this way, choice pollutes and curses you and everyone around you (like Eve did to Adam, when she used her choice to eat the fruit and not only cursed herself, but the one she loved most). Choice is powerful, and when something so powerful is wielded so carelessly, it is dangerous. But when something so powerful is wielded correctly and selflessly, it has the potential to change the world.

So…Let's use our gift of choice to change and transform the world.

<u>Colossians 1:6</u>

New Living Translation (NLT)

6 This same Good News that came to you is going out all over the world. It is bearing fruit everywhere by changing lives, just as it changed your lives from the day you first heard and understood the truth about God's wonderful grace.

JEALOUSY: THE GATEWAY SIN

Once upon a time, in a land not far from yours,
there was a girl and her father:

"Daughter, do you know which of the sins is the most
dangerous?" The father asked. "No. Which is it?" The daughter
asked in return. "Jealousy." The father answered. "Why?"
the daughter asked. "Because jealousy will turn you into a
person you no longer recognize." The father answered.

The dictionary defines **jealousy** as: *resentment against
a rival, a person enjoying success or advantage, or
against another's success or advantage itself.*

Jealousy is a seed.

A seed has potential for tremendous growth and reproduction
when planted under the right conditions. When we start to
have feelings of jealousy towards someone (and leave them
unchecked), that one seed of jealousy turns into a tree, and that
one tree has the potential to turn into a forest. This is why it is
important to catch jealousy at its inception, before it has had a
chance to grow. Because after it has grown, instead of having
to just dig out the roots of one tree when trying to uproot
jealousy, we now have to dig out the roots of an entire forest!

That's what's so deadly about jealousy, it grows, and you can't
stop the growth unless you dig out the roots. I repeat: DIG OUT
THE ROOTS! That's the only way to get rid of jealousy. Otherwise,
your one seed of jealousy will turn into a forest of hate, envy,
and eventually murder. Now this murder isn't always in the
physical sense (but we have all heard of stories in which jealousy
has turned into actual physical murder), but what's even more
dangerous is that this murder can be in the spiritual sense, the
emotional sense and even the social sense. While in the grips of
jealousy, we start to bad mouth the people that we are jealous
of and kill them in the eyes of the people they love most.

Another disturbing quality about jealousy, is in most cases the person that we are jealous of, isn't even aware of the hate and envy that we harbor inside of ourselves toward them. So, while our jealousy seed continues to grow into a forest of murder, this person, the subject of our jealousy is loving us, unaware of the threat; of the murder that is lurking beneath the Christian standing before their very eyes.

This hate, this murder, is another way in which jealousy is so harmful, because it causes us to kill the innocent. After jealousy has led us to murder someone we know is innocent, we start to slowly die off from the rot starting to form within our decaying forest, grown from a single seed of jealousy. Our forest starts to rot because now that we have murdered the source of its growth (our jealousy), the forest no longer has anything to sustain itself on, and begins to decay. It begins to rot. And if something is rotten it dies; we die.

Proverbs 14:30
New International Version (NIV)
*A heart at peace gives life to the body, but **envy rots** the bones.*

To sum up the gateway of sin that jealousy can lead us through and to, can be shown in this way:

Jealousy –> Envy –> Hate –> Murder –> Death

People often use jealousy and envy interchangeably, but they are different words with different meanings. Jealousy comes first in line because it _begins_ with the resentment of something someone else has. Envy is defined as the *"painful awareness"* of something someone else has. It means that this feeling has _grown_ from discomfort to actual pain, and the chain just continues from there.

I think the best thing that we can do when confronted with jealousy at its inception, is to first actively recognize it for what it is, with the intent to kill this seed. It is only after we have made this honest acknowledgment of what it is, that we can begin to overcome our jealousy. We need to take the object or mannerism about this person that makes us jealous and try to see it as God would see it, _or_ counter it with something that we really like about this person and focus our energies only on that, until we can no longer see this "thing" inside of them (or the things which they have) which makes us jealous.

We mustn't let a seed of jealousy towards another turn into death for ourselves. We have chosen to be Christians; no one has forced us to accept Christ. We did that all on our own. So, let's start walking in Him and with Him. When we are walking in Christ and with Christ, we are walking in Love and with Love and...

<u>Love can never be jealous.</u>

1 Corinthians 13:3-8

Contemporary English Version (CEV)

[3] What if I gave away all that I owned and let myself be burned alive? I would gain nothing, unless I loved others. [4] Love is kind and patient, **never jealous**, boastful, proud, or [5] rude. Love isn't selfish or quick tempered. It doesn't keep a record of wrongs that others do. [6] Love rejoices in the truth, but not in evil. [7] Love is always supportive, loyal, hopeful, and trusting. [8] Love never fails!

THE ANTIBIOTIC FOR FEAR

Once upon a time, in a land not far from yours
there was a girl and her father:

"Father", the daughter said. "I think I've figured out
the secret to inner peace". "What is it?" the father
asked. "Trust" the daughter answered.

In the midst of another one of my "dark" days, I was trying to
rationalize myself into a good mood (no matter what people
say, THIS DOESN'T WORK). So I started soul searching and
mind searching; both horribly dangerous tasks to do especially
during the middle of the work day, but you know us "in-our-
head" types, anytime is the perfect time for an existential crisis.
But, to get back on topic, during my "quest" I found something
inside of me; something terrifying and alarming. I found Fear!

(Queue scary music: dun, dun, dun!)

I'm not talking about bungee jumping or cliff diving Fear, I'm
talking about deeply-rooted, driving-force Fear. I found that
Fear has been one of the primary driving forces of my life since
my younger years. I'll even go as far as to say that fear has been
driving me since the development of my conscious self.

I think that if you have been one of those "fortunate" people
to have been introduced to Christianity in your infancy
(more than introduced, more like forced), then you were
raised with a different lens by which to view the world.
A lens which your parents and religious environment
upon your birth gifted you with; a lens of Fear. This lens
shows you the most dire of consequences associated with
the most trivial offenses. While growing up, this seemed
to be the only lens with which I was "blessed".

Christianity for me as a child was hard, unyielding and
unforgiving. I was taught that if you knew better and did it

anyway, there was no salvation or redemption for you; that God would write you off and give you a one-way ticket to hell. So, for me, this meant that I couldn't mess up or make a mistake "or else". And, this is how I continued my life for a long time, in Fear, doing all that I could to avoid God's wrath and punishment by staying on "good behavior".

It wasn't until some years ago that I realized, that it was my Love of God that made me not want to sin; not my Fear of Him. But even long after that day of great revelation, the residual of a Fear once so great was still left behind, like the hidden mutated strains of an infection you once thought cured. This Fear of punishment and retribution from God for my sins took on a new form; The Fear of Failure. This one abhorrent piece of my humanity haunts me incessantly. No matter how hard I've tried to "treat" it, and cure myself of it, Fear still thrives. I'm extremely critical of and hard on myself, always convinced that I can do better; that I can do more.

It was amid these feelings that I found fear hiding and thriving deep within me. This presented me with both a breakthrough and a conundrum. So, now that I've found the "root" cause of my mental unrest and hindrance to inner peace, how do I fix it? I know the typical Christian answer: fast and pray for God to take it out of you. But now I ask, how can I ask God to take out of me what my religion has placed within me? And then I remembered the scripture **2 Timothy 1:7**: *For God hath not given us the spirit of fear; but of power, and of love, and of a **sound mind.***

Okay, so now I have a scripture which helped soothed my wounds, but just reading and remembering these biblical words didn't heal them. So, I really contemplated the scripture for a while, and came away with three things.

Number one: God has not given me the spirit of Fear, but I have it.

Number two: I would really like to get to

the sound mind part, <u>but how</u>?

<u>Number three</u>: The words "Trust God" kept coming to mind.

Then another scripture came to me: **Proverbs 3:5-6** *Trust in the Lord with all your heart, and lean not on your own understanding; in all your ways acknowledge Him and He shall direct your paths.*

I started to comprehend these words for what they really are, and dropped the mundane clichés so often attached to them. I started to think that to Trust God and in order to actually be able to benefit from it, I would need to Trust God implicitly, against all logic and reason. I repeated this to myself again: "against ALL logic and reason". I understand that on paper this sounds easy, but in practice this is insanely hard.

I realized that if I could really Trust God in this way, the Fear which I harbored could no longer thrive inside of me. I realized that the Antibiotic for Fear is Trust.

I've experienced this kind of trust in my familial and marital relationships, but not completely in the spiritual sense. For example, I trust my spouse and since I trust my spouse I am not afraid (fearful), that my spouse will cheat on me.

After thinking of this, I had to ask myself if I truly trust God? Well, of course, I trust in God, but maybe not completely; maybe not in the way a textbook Christian should. I still have the fear, that if *I* don't do things right, then things will not turn out well for me. I think that as a flesh-wrapped-human being, it's hard not to try to be in control of every aspect of your life. You start to feel that it is your talents, gifts and work ethic that will make you successful in life, and while in part that is true, as a Christian there is also one more component: Faith.

This is where Faith popped in and made me realize that it is not only important, but an integral part in being a Christian. If we are without Faith, then we are without hope, and without hope, we are without a reason to live, and without a reason to live, we are without life.

Trust is Faith and Faith is Life.

After many years I've found the key to inner peace. For me it's not prayer, or fasting, or reading the bible, or even going to church every Sunday (even though all these ways are ways are helpful); it's pure, simple, difficult-to-attain, COMPLETE Trust in God. I hope that one day I can reach this place.

Psalms 22:9-10

English Standard Version (ESV)

Yet you are he who took me from the womb;
you made me trust you at my mother's breasts.
¹⁰On you was I cast from my birth,
and from my mother's womb you have been my God.

Psalms 37:3-4

English Standard Version (ESV)

IS THERE REALLY A POINT OF NO RETURN?

Once upon a time, in a land not far from yours,
there was a girl and her father:

"Daughter…" the father began one day. "…remember that if you resist the devil, he will flee. Otherwise, if you keep playing with him, he's going to keep playing with you." The father warned.

Is there truly such a point as no return? Is there such a point where once you've gone too far, there's no turning back? Is there such a situation where once you've started, it's too late? Or, have you ever heard someone give the excuse, "it just happened"?

At what point do we let go of conscience, and let emotions override? Is there really no way out in the "heat of the moment" or are we just unaware of how to escape?

At some point as Christians, we have to be careful of the things and situations that we allow ourselves to get into. Like they say in medicine, "prevention is the best cure". In the spiritual case, I would translate that to "declination thwarts temptation".

If we can learn to say no early on, our risk of falling into temptation would drop considerably. As Christians, we all have God's spirit dwelling inside of us. It is His spirit that automatically alerts us when we are about to encounter "enemy territory", long before we cross over into it. I believe that recognizing the early warning signs of impending temptation is an integral part in overcoming it.

We all know the early warning signs of getting close to temptation. First, there is an overwhelming uneasiness that we either choose to listen to or ignore. Next, is apprehension coupled with guilt for entertaining the notion. Lastly, we snowball into a plethora of mixed emotions that make us so uncomfortable we want to crawl out of our own skin. This is why I think it is so important to turn away from "iffy" situations before they evolve into temptation.

Now on the other hand, if we have already crossed over into "enemy territory" and are immediately confronted with our temptation (and see no way out) my advice... Run! You'd be amazed at how well this works! It is better to seem like a coward before men, than to sin "knowingly" before God. We must internalize our Christian beliefs to make our walk with Christ worthwhile. Otherwise, why constantly deny ourselves if we are unsure of our beliefs in the power and peace of God?

I believe that no such "point" exists. I believe that there is always a way out of something that you've gotten yourself into. I believe in the possibility of turning things around. I believe that as Christians, we don't put our Faith in lost causes. I believe that no matter how far that you have walked down that wrong road, it is always possible to find your way back and start over.

<u>1 Corinthians 10:12-13</u>

New Living Translation (NLT)

12 If you think you are standing strong, be careful not to fall. 13 The temptations in your life are no different from what others experience. And God is faithful. He will not allow the temptation to be more than you can stand. When you are tempted, He will show you a way out so that you can endure.

As Christians there is no such thing as a point of no return, because as the scripture states: He will show you a way out so that you can endure.

So, I say, let's endure together.

EVERYBODY LIES?

Once upon a time in a land not far from yours,
there was a girl and her father:

"Daughter, did you take extra cookies out of the cookie jar?" the father asked. "No." the girl waveringly answered. "Go and get the bible, and open it to Proverbs 6:16-17", the father commanded. "What does it say?" The father asked once the book was opened. The girl began to read, *"There are six things the LORD hates, seven that are detestable to him: haughty eyes, a lying tongue..."* "Stop right there and put your hand on the bible over the passage." The father instructed. The girl did as she was told. "Now, your hand is on God's word, and if you lie, you not only lie to me, but to God also. So, I'm going to ask you again daughter, did you take the cookies?" the father asked. "Yes." The girl answered.

Do you lie? And if you do lie, do you rate your lies? Some people rate their lies based on colors such as little white lies and some rate their lies based on consequence, but in reality, do lies have ratings? Or, are lies just lies? As Christians we are charged with living a lifestyle free of deceit and lies. This charge is evidenced by the Proverbs scripture listed above and there are many other such examples in the bible just to name a few: Psalms 5:5-6 *...You hate all who do wrong; You destroy those who tell lies..."* and Leviticus 19:11 *...Do not lie. Do not deceive one another."*

Yet even, in reading and knowing all of this, why do we lie? Do we think that we can get away with it? Do we consider lying to be a tiny sin compared to all the others out there? Do we think that small offenses in comparison to larger ones, have a similarly assigned consequence? Do we lie to make ourselves look great in front of others? Do we lie to hide the secrets about ourselves? Or, have some of us "learned" to tell the truth to avoid lying outright; what some would call a lie of omission?

I had a co-worker once ask me, "Doesn't everybody lie?" I wanted to answer, "No!" I wanted to be able to give the ideal answer that "Christians don't lie because it is against our Faith and our religion", but I couldn't. All that I could tell him was that there are people out there that don't believe in lying and choose not to.

Our Faith must mean more to us and be stronger than our lusts of the flesh; in particular, our want to lie. Merely being educated about the harmful effects of lies is not enough to stop us from lying. We must internalize this ideal in the same way that we internalize our Faith and Love of God. Unbelievably in some instances, the threat of Hell alone is not enough to deter us from doing this. It's funny how as Christians, we have a talent for rationalizing away the threat of Hell when we are faced with our sins. But we have to start accepting our sins, and actively try to change the way that we live our lives.

If the fear of Hell isn't enough to get us to stop lying, then our Love of God should be. I understand that we're human, and that we like to make allowances for our humanity but at some point, enough is enough! Are we going to walk with God, or aren't we? Let's be the Christians that we should be, the Christians we believe that we can be, and the Christians that God expects for us to be. We are supposed to be the lights of the world, so let's allow our light to burn bright; fueled by truth and the boldness to tell it. Let's start to lead the way and lead it honestly.

Revelations 21:8

New Living Translation (NLT)

*8 "But cowards, unbelievers, the corrupt, murderers, the immoral, those who practice witchcraft, idol worshipers, and all **liars**—their fate is in the fiery lake of burning sulfur. This is the second death."*

<u>1Peter 3:10</u>

New Living Translation (NLT)

[10] *For the Scriptures say, "If you want to enjoy life and see many happy days, keep your tongue from speaking evil and your lips from telling lies.*

GOD'S FORGIVENESS, NOT MAN'S, IS ALL THAT MATTERS

Once upon a time, in a land not far from yours,
there was a girl and her father:

"Daughter I have noticed something as I have gotten older." The father said. "What's that?" the daughter asked. "That a lot of us go around our whole lives feeling guilty because the people that we have hurt won't forgive us. But, I have realized that the only forgiveness that we need to be free, is God's." the father answered.

At some point in our lives (Pre-Christian or Post-Christian) we have hurt someone else with our actions and/or words. Usually some time later, once we have calmed down and realized that we have hurt someone and created an issue which could have been avoided, we feel bad. Guilty, even. These bad feelings and guilt lead us to seek forgiveness for our actions.

Seeking forgiveness is a two-part process. First, we must seek forgiveness from God, and then the person which we have hurt. I guess the asking forgiveness part from God is the easiest because we are sure of His love for us, and even though we come to Him in shame over our actions, we know that after we have "sincerely" repented He will forgive us our sin of hurting another.

Nehemiah 9:17

New Living Translation (NLT)

[17] *… But you are a God of forgiveness, gracious and merciful, slow to become angry, and rich in unfailing love…*

However, part two seems to be the most difficult. The part of actually and physically facing the person we have hurt and asking them for forgiveness in the midst of their pain. I think this part is the most difficult because there are no guarantees that they will forgive us. And when we have realized our wrong and are trying to make it right, and our attempts at apology and asking forgiveness are not welcomed with open arms, this can leave us feeling many things. We feel more guilt and sadness over not being forgiven by this person. We may even feel anger over the fact that they won't accept our attempt at doing the right thing and reciprocate our Godly action.

<u>But the truth is</u>: They don't have to forgive us for us to be free.

Yes. It would be nice to be forgiven, given that in most cases we might see the person either frequently or intermittently as we go about our daily lives. And that in seeing them, we are reminded of the deeds that have passed between us both, which makes us feel the guilt and sadness all over again. But what I am trying to say is that we don't have to feel this way. God's forgiveness is the only forgiveness that we need. If the person that we hurt is unwilling to forgive us in return, then that is between them and God.

Matthew 6:14–15

New Living Translation (NLT)

[14] *"If you forgive those who sin against you, your heavenly Father will forgive you.* [15] *But if you refuse to forgive others, your Father will not forgive your sins.*

Now, I'm not saying that we only ask God's forgiveness, and completely leave the person that we have hurt out of it; dismissing their feelings. As I have mentioned above: forgiveness is a two-part process. Once we have completed both parts, we are free and should live and walk in the freedom of forgiveness. When we decide to walk in the freedom of forgiveness, we are free from the guilt, the sadness, and the depression of the consequences of our sin. This freedom can only happen if we let it go and forgive ourselves as God has forgiven us (whether the person that we have hurt has forgiven us or not). Our only duty after we have sought forgiveness is to still Love, whether the person we have hurt decides to reciprocate that love or not.

Proverbs 17:9

New Living Translation (NLT)
Love prospers when a fault is forgiven, but
dwelling on it separates close friends

I believe this Love which we show is how we prove to God that we are sincere in asking forgiveness, but not only that. By giving Love to the person that we hurt (whether they have forgiven us or not), proves the existence of God's Love in us. As I am always saying, we are representatives for Christ. This doesn't mean that we will never mess up, but when we do, this shouldn't stop us from being representatives for Him, or deter us from striving to be like Him. If our mess up involves another person, then let us "fix it up" with God's Love towards them. There is forgiveness for us all if we just ask…and Love.

Luke 7:47

Amplified Bible (AMP)

[47] *Therefore I tell you, her sins, many [as they are], are forgiven her—because she has loved much. But he who is forgiven little loves little.*

HOPE THAT IS SEEN IS NO HOPE AT ALL

Once upon a time, in a land not far from yours,
there was a girl and her father:

"Father, I've done everything right, and yet it seems
that everything is falling apart! Why?" the daughter
asked. "Remember that God is in control. Don't worry
because your worry won't fix anything. You have to
Trust God. All things work together for the good, for
those who love God." The father answered.

Recently, I've had to really reach deep and pull out all my
Faith and Trust God. Sometimes in our lives, unexpected
things happen that leave us with no choice but to rely on
God. I think that God presents us with these situations on
purpose to see what we will do. To see if we will Trust Him.

As a human you want to worry, stress, rant and rave about
the unexpected situations that have landed into your lap. We
figure that if we just keep doing things _right,_ everything will
fall into place as we expect it. But I think that we have all been
Christians long enough to know that it doesn't work that way.

We can plan as much as we want, make all the "right" moves,
but in the end the path that our life takes, is up to God. When
we decided to give our Souls over to Christ and to Trust
completely in Him, our path changed. Our path became God's
path, and we have to believe, know, and Trust that all things
are working together for our own good. Remember that God
will create that path for us, that will lead us to true happiness;
that will lead us to realized dreams long forgotten.

I wanted to share this passage of scripture with you,
because it is giving me hope when I can see no way out,

and when I become confused or disappointed.

<u>Romans 8:24-30</u>

New International Version (NIV)

24 For in this hope we were saved. But hope that is seen is no hope at all. Who hopes for what they already have? 25 But if we hope for what we do not yet have, we wait for it patiently.

26 In the same way, the Spirit helps us in our weakness. We do not know what we ought to pray for, but the Spirit himself intercedes for us through wordless groans. 27 And he who searches our hearts knows the mind of the Spirit, because the Spirit intercedes for God's people in accordance with the will of God.

28 And we know that in all things God works for the good of those who love him, who have been called according to his purpose. 29 For those God foreknew he also predestined to be conformed to the image of his Son, that he might be the firstborn among many brothers and sisters. 30And those he predestined, he also called; those he called, he also justified; those he justified, he also glorified.

HOT? COLD? OR LUKEWARM?

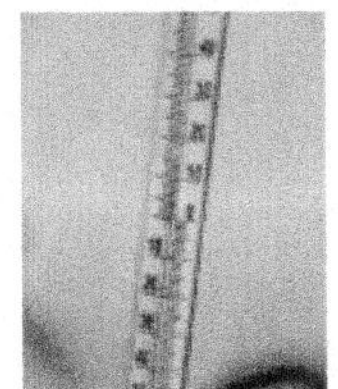

Once upon a time, in a land not far from yours,
there was a girl and her father:

"Daughter, a man cannot serve two masters", the father said. "Why do you say that father?" the girl asked. "Because, there is going to be a point in your life where you will have to choose between God and yourself. You cannot serve both; otherwise you will be forever tormented." The father returned.

If we have been Christians for some time, we have all heard of, or read about being Hot, Cold, or Lukewarm. If this concept is new to you, the scripture which I am referring to is **Revelation 3:15-16** (NLT) [15] *"I know all the things you do, that you are neither hot nor cold. I wish that you were one or the other!* [16] *But since you are like lukewarm water, neither hot nor cold, I will spit you out of my mouth!*

What does this mean? The common interpretation is that either you serve God with your whole heart, in beliefs, and deeds (Hot); or don't serve God at all in anyway (Cold). The problem that we most commonly see in the members of our Faith (and sometime in ourselves as well), is the tendency for us to be Lukewarm; a mixture of hot and cold. This means that half of ourselves is dedicated to God, while the other half is dedicated to some other master (usually ourselves).

Is it not a wonder that we are all so confused and so conflicted? It is painful and impossible to find peace while trying to serve two masters (these two masters being ourselves and God). I think that God is trying to convey more to us in this scripture, than just His displeasure towards us as lukewarm mixtures of ourselves and our Faith. I think that He is trying to save us from our own personal Hells which we create for ourselves.

We must choose to serve one master and do so faithfully or else we will never find peace. We have perfect examples of Hot and Cold in our everyday lives. At some point in our Christian walk, we have been acquainted with unbelievers that can't be happier with the current state of their lives. They are balanced and at peace with the god which they have decided to serve; themselves. Conversely, we have encountered "Real" Christians (in the spiritual sense, not the doctrinal sense). The ones that epitomize what Christianity is all about, and we have seen how they are at peace and happy in their Faith.

I think that at the end of the day, what it comes down to is the battle between our Spirit and our Flesh. Our Spirit wants to be closer to God, to walk with Him, and in Him, and experience that spiritual oneness and peace. But, on the other hand, our Flesh wants to be recognized and satisfied, and it won't allow us to be at peace or find comfort within ourselves until "*It*" gets what it wants.

Sometimes it's not about trying to find a balance between the Flesh and the Spirit (Lukewarm). Sometimes it is about choosing one or the other. Being Hot or Cold. At some point we have to decide if this Faith is for us, and whether or not we are going to dedicate our lives to one Master, to one Faith and to one Truth. As Christians, let's choose to be Hot, and spend every day trying to turn off that inner Cold faucet, until the only faucet left running water is Hot.

Matthew 5:29-30

New Living Translation (NLT)

[29] So if your eye—even your good eye—causes you to lust, gouge it out and throw it away. It is better for you to lose one part of your body than for your whole body to be thrown into hell. [30] And

*if your hand—even your stronger hand—causes you to sin, cut
it off and throw it away. It is better for you to lose one part of
your body than for your whole body to be thrown into hell.*

IF YOU CAN'T SEE IT FAITH IT AND WATCH GOD MOVE

Once upon a time, in a land not far from yours,
there was a girl and her father:

"Dad, I'm stressed out! There's no money and I don't
know how I'm going to pay these bills!" the daughter
complained. "You need to have Faith." The Father replied.
"That sounds nice dad, but I still don't see how I'm going
to pay these bills!" "You're not supposed to see it daughter.
That's why it's called Faith." The father replied.

Have you ever had those times where you just didn't see
a way out? You know, the times where we worry and try
to figure things out? When we feel like if we could just
crunch those numbers one more time, we will finally get
the desired result? Or, if we dissect a situation enough, we
can get to the real root of the problem and then solve it?

Now sometimes these works are necessary to everyday
life, and can make things easier. But sometimes we might
follow all the right steps, and still not come up with
the desired result. When this happens, we have to stop
trying to see a way out and begin to trust in God.

It's called Faith...

Hebrews 11:1

King James Version (KJV)

*11 Now faith is the substance of things hoped
for, the evidence of things not seen.*

Faith is the essence of our walk with God. None of us
have ever seen Him, but we still feel and believe that
He is. Christianity is Faith, and we have to apply our
Christianity to our lives; to our everyday walk. We have to

believe that God is looking out for us, and we don't have to see a way out, to believe that God will see us out.

Have Faith. If you can't see it, Faith it and watch God move…

IT'LL BE OK, JUST GET THROUGH TODAY

Once upon a time, in a land not far from yours,
there was a girl and her father:

"Father, this is just too hard, I don't think I am going to make it." Cried the daughter, feeling defeated. "Just keep putting one foot in front of the other, and you will be amazed at how far you will go. Walk in Trust, walk in Faith, and let the Lord direct your path." The Father responded.

Sometimes it's hard to remember that today is just a drop in the bucket, compared to all the days that we will live through in our entire life time. But even with that knowledge in the back of our heads, sometimes it is hard to keep that perspective when you feel as if you are struggling just to get through minutes to make it to the next hour. We've all had those days where we have felt like our life has ended, or that our entire future success has been compromised.

I once took a class with a psychologist who said: *there are our thoughts on a situation, and then there is the truth of a situation.* Sometimes it is hard…no, nearly impossible to see past our thoughts to the truth. This can be dangerous because one day our thoughts will become the things which make our lives. If we keep having and holding onto the negative thoughts day after day after day; this one bad day can *potentially* turn into a bad lifetime.

I have an aunt that always says, you're not having a bad day, you're having a bad moment. For example, if you wake up out of bed and stub your toe, that is a bad moment. Do not fret over this moment and let it become your day. The morning might not have started out well in that particular moment, but you do not have to carry that with you throughout your day. Move on to the other challenges which the day will provide, and walk in Faith knowing that everything which is happening is working out in your favor (even the bad moments).

<u>Romans 8:28</u>

New International Version (NIV)

²⁸And we know that in all things God works for the good of those who love him, who have been called according to his purpose.

You might think, "yeah, sure, easier said than done" and you are right! It is much easier to say these things than to do them. This is where our Faith comes in. If it is too difficult for you to see how you are going to make it, stick to the old age advice of "a day at a time" and mix it with a little Faith. If you can find that mustard-seed-sized-Faith, and keep waking up day after day, things will get better. Things will start to make sense again. You will begin to hope again; dream again.

Each day is a new beginning, a new hope, a second chance. We must lean on God and stay encouraged. If we lean on God and let *those* thoughts become things, we will be rewarded with light at the end of our tunnels.

<u>Jeremiah 29:11-13</u>

Contemporary English Version (CEV)

¹¹I will bless you with a future filled with hope—a future of success, not of suffering. ¹²You will turn back to me and ask for help, and I will answer your prayers. ¹³You will worship me with all your heart, and I will be with you.

MVP (MOST VALUABLE POSSESSION)

Once upon a time, in a land not far from yours
there was a girl and her father:

"Father what is the most valuable thing we own? Is it our
money? Is it our house?" the girl asked. "No, the most
valuable things which we own aren't our money or our
house." The father answered. "Then what is it father?"
the girl asked. "Our Souls", the father answered.

They say that we are born into this world with nothing, and that
when we die we can't take anything with us, but I beg to differ.
We are born into this world with something, and when we leave
this world behind, we take it with us. "What is this thing?" you
might ask. This "thing" is our Soul. Our Soul is ours and only
ours, and what makes it our most valuable possession is that
it can't be taken; it can only be given, and given willingly.

Our soul is immaterial. It can't be "physically" bought or
sold. We can't collect them or show them off. We can't
touch them, but we can *feel* them. The Soul can never die.
In **Matthew 10:28** it says, *"Don't be afraid of those who
want to kill your body; they cannot touch your soul."*

We can starve our soul, or we can feed it. We can nurture
it, or we can neglect it. Our Soul is the essence of who
we are. The Soul is the source of all valuable things
immaterial. Our Soul is the source of our ability to Love
one another, to forgive those that trespass against us, and
our center for peace and "spiritual" understanding.

But, as Christians, do we really know the true value of our
Soul? In **Matthew 16:26** it says *"And what do you benefit if you
gain the whole world but lose your own soul? Is anything worth
more than your soul?"* and again in **Mark 8:37** *"Is anything worth*

more than your soul?" Don't the words of the scripture seem to resonate within you? Is anything worth more than your soul?

Have you ever heard of someone selling their soul to the devil? Haven't you ever wondered why of all the things which we personally own, the devil only wants our soul in return for the "ultimate" favor (to be famous, to make someone love us, to be rich)? The devil also knows that our soul is our most valuable and powerful possession, and that when we give it over to God, that he can't touch us; that he can never own us. This is the spiritual warfare which we hear so much about, it is the war between God and the devil fighting over our souls.

We have been given a gift of choice. No one can make us choose one over the other. We get to choose if we want to give our souls over to God and live in Him, or to the devil and live in him.

And yet, there still is another option that I have failed to mention. You could always keep your soul for yourself. You can live for yourself, and no one else. But, I guess here is where our Faith comes in. Do we really want to spend our short span of existence totally engrossed in ourselves? And conversely, do we really want to spend our entire existence engrossed in a cause outside of ourselves?

This can be a difficult decision to make because it makes us ask ourselves who do we love more: Ourselves or God?

So, I guess the big question is: Who do you chose to give your most valuable possession to?

Luke 12:33-34

English Standard Version (ESV)

33 Sell your possessions, and give to the needy. Provide yourselves with moneybags that do not grow old, with a treasure in the heavens *that does not fail, where no thief approaches and no moth destroys. 34 For where your treasure is, there will your heart be also.*

SELFISHNESS IS SATANIC?

Once upon a time in a land not far from yours
there was a girl and her father:

"Daughter, one of our most important responsibilities
as Christians is to Love everyone." the father said.
"Everyone, father?" the daughter asked. "Yes, everyone.
We are to love everyone because we are all God's
creatures and by loving one another, we fulfill God's
purpose here on Earth." The father answered.

Some years ago, I took a class on the anthropology of religion.
What I remembered most from this class was the final
research paper I had to turn in. For this research paper each
student was able to choose a religion which they wanted to
know more about, different from their current religion (if
they practiced one). So out of the list given to us of possible
religions to research, I chose satanism. Yes, satanism.

I think as Christians we sometimes give too much power to
the devil in the form of fear. One of the biggest ways in which
to combat fear is through knowledge, and conversely one of
the biggest ways to allow fear to thrive and over take us is
ignorance. I often see in our religion, that to learn of satan is
considered taboo. This taboo seems to hold that if we learn of
satan and his ways, somehow "he" will enter our souls, and
that's just not true. Now, I'm not suggesting that we go into
intensive study of satanism and learn all of the intricate inner
workings of it. All that I am trying to convey is that we need
to know his agenda, so that we know how to battle, fight, and
thwart his agenda. In this way we can help bring more souls to
Christ, and continue to light up the world with God's Love.

The most surprising and important thing that I learned

about Satanism was that the foundation of this religion and its practices center around **selfishness.** It's about looking out for yourself, no matter the cost that it brings (even at the expense of others). satanism teaches that you are the center of your universe, and that looking out for, and always pleasing "#1" (yourself) is paramount. Doesn't sound too Satanic does it? But, let's think about this for a moment. What are the characteristics of the selfish person?

The synonyms for selfishness are: greed, self-centeredness, self-indulgence, **self-worship**, and stinginess. Just to name a few.

A selfish person will do "anything" to get ahead and further their own agenda. Selfish people make war. They kill, steal, and destroy to gain what it is they want.

(Now that is starting to sound satanic)

John 10:9-11

New King James Version (NKJV)

⁹I am the door. If anyone enters by Me, he will be saved, and will go in and out and find pasture. ¹⁰The thief does not come except to steal, and to kill, and to destroy. I have come that they may have life, and that they may have it more abundantly. ¹¹"I am the good shepherd. The good shepherd <u>gives His life for the sheep.</u>

Remember that selfishness is not a stand alone quality, similar to the jealousy piece I wrote about previously. Selfishness will lead you into more sinful (and satanic) places.

James 3:16

Amplified Bible (AMP)
*16 For wherever there is jealousy (envy) and contention (rivalry and **selfish** ambition), there will also be confusion (unrest,*

disharmony, rebellion) and all sorts of evil and vile practices.

This scripture shows how thoughts and feelings of selfishness (selfish ambition) will eventually lead into *all sorts of evil and vile practices.*

But the interesting thing about selfishness is that the seed of it is rooted inside of our humanity. We all have things that we don't want to share. Things which we believe belong exclusively to us so we don't *have* to share them. Somehow and in some ways, we allow ourselves selfishness, as if it's this need inside of us we have to feed. But, what I'm trying to convey in this reading is that selfishness is the root of all evil; that selfishness is satanic.

I know what I've written seems like it goes against the scripture, but look closely. When you look up the synonym for selfishness, greed appears; and when you look up the synonym for greed, selfishness appears. They are one and the same. Different words which convey the same sentiment. This is why I say that selfishness is the root of all evil because selfishness needs to be present in order for greed to take root.

Psalm 10:3-8

Amplified Bible (AMP)

*[3] For the wicked man boasts (sings the praises) of **his own** heart's desire, and the one **greedy for gain** curses and spurns, yes, renounces and despises the Lord... [4] The wicked one in the pride of **his countenance** will not seek, inquire for, and yearn for God; **all his thoughts** are that there is no God... [7] **his mouth** is full of cursing, deceit, oppression (fraud); under his tongue are trouble and sin (mischief and iniquity). [8] **he sits** in ambush in the villages; in hiding places **he slays the innocent; he watches stealthily** for the poor (the helpless and unfortunate).*

Satanism doesn't focus on the Devil, as much as it focuses

on the importance of relying on self, and indulging in yourself (the flesh). It focuses on personal happiness and not spiritual harmony with yourself **and** others.

<u>Our fight against selfishness (satanism) is a fight against our human nature. We can only overcome this nature with Love for one another and complete trust in God.</u>

<u>Philippians 2:3-5</u>

Amplified Bible (AMP)

*³Do nothing from factional motives [through contentiousness, strife, **selfishness**, or for unworthy ends] or prompted by conceit and empty arrogance. Instead, in the true spirit of humility (**lowliness of mind**) let each regard the others as better than and superior to himself [thinking more highly of one another than you do of yourselves]. ⁴Let each of you esteem and look upon and **be concerned for not [merely] his own interests, but also each for the interests of others.** ⁵Let this same attitude and purpose and [humble] mind be in you which was in Christ Jesus: [Let Him be your example in humility:]*

<u>John 5:30</u>

Amplified Bible (AMP)

*³⁰**I am able to do nothing from Myself** [independently, of My own accord—but only as I am taught by God and as I get His orders]. Even as I hear, I judge [I decide as I am bidden to decide. As the voice comes to Me, so I give a decision], and My judgment is right (just, righteous), **because I do not seek or consult My own will [I have no desire to do what is pleasing to Myself, My own aim, My own purpose]** but only the will and pleasure of the Father Who sent Me.*

Jesus is our great Christian example.

<u>Hebrews 4:15-16</u>

New Living Translation (NLT)

*¹⁵ This High Priest of ours understands our weaknesses, for he faced all of the same testings we do, **yet he did not sin**.*

Jesus refused to sin, not only because He considered himself above it, but because He knew that sin would lead Him away from His Father and instead lead Him towards the path of satan. The best thing that we could ever do for ourselves, our souls, and our God is to not feed our flesh. Do not indulge in selfish pleasures. Being a Christian is so much bigger than Heaven and Hell. It's about choosing a side in this spiritual warfare and doing our work as soldiers for God; being undiminished lights for God, and removing the darkness of ignorance that the devil has tried to place our world in. I hope and pray that we all continue to be lights, examples, and representatives of Christ in this fallen world.

Let's start to do things for ourselves that are not only good for ourselves but also for others. In this way, satan does not get any of the glory. In this way, all of the glory goes to God.

Galatians 5:13-14

Amplified Bible (AMP)

13 For you, brethren, were [indeed] called to freedom; only [do not let your] freedom be an incentive to your flesh and an opportunity or excuse [for selfishness], but through love you should serve one another.

GIVING PEOPLE WHAT THEY DON'T DESERVE

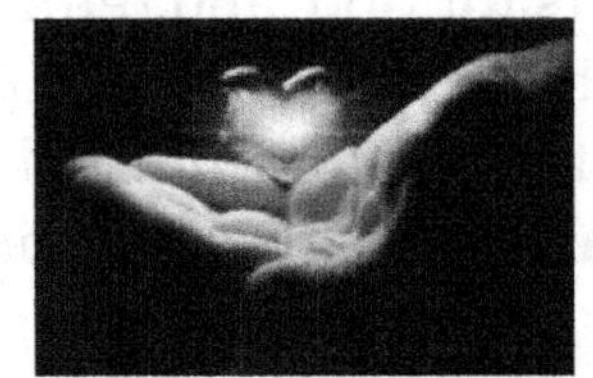

Once upon a time, in a land not far from yours,
there was a girl and her father:

"Daughter, if you don't want to visit your sick friend because
of the mean things she did to you in the past, I won't force
you." The father said. "I know father. But, I also know that
I should visit her, and visit with her happily." The girl said.
"Why is that?" the father asked. "Because I am a Christian and
God has told me to Love and show Love. It's not up to me to
decide whether or not she deserves it." The girl answered.

Yes, this concept sounds unfair and illogical, which is why it
is spiritual. In a previous post I published, I wrote about how
selfishness is satanic, and why it is important to our Christian
Faith to banish away all selfishness. I

also wrote about how in the satanic text, it is written that
you should only do good to people and respect people that
do good to you and respect you. This is how many of us
Christians are deceived. The devil will hide his agenda under
man's logic, and that's when we become confused.

Sometimes we may think, "if it makes sense and seems fair, it
must be of God, right?" I'm writing today to tell you that the
answer to this question is "*No!*". This is why we must study
our bibles so that we not only recognize the devil's tricks, but
also so that "we ourselves" know what it is to be Christian,
and not what someone else tells us "Christian" should be.

It is our duty as Christians to Love and do good unto everyone,
regardless of their feelings and actions toward us. Now, this
does not mean that we should just turn over and be taken
advantage of with our eyes open. Rather, it means that we should
show love and respect to all, not because they deserve it, but

because we are Christians. It is our duty to Love one another, and not judge one another. It is not up to us to decide whether a person is deserving of our brotherly Love towards them.

I repeat: Our duty is to Love; not to judge. Remember that we are representatives of Christ, and that His spirit dwells in us. I think the Apostle Luke says it best in this passage of scripture, that we all as Christians should internalize and live by. This scripture also illustrates why we need to continually make it our duty to follow God's word *"1st"*, and not only man's logic. What I'm trying to convey is that God continuously gives us graces and love that we don't deserve, so why can't we do the same for our fellow man?

Luke 6:27-37 (New International Version)

[27] *"But to you who are listening I say: Love your enemies, do good to those who hate you,* [28] *bless those who curse you, pray for those who mistreat you.* [29] *If someone slaps you on one cheek, turn to them the other also. If someone takes your coat, do not withhold your shirt from them.* [30] *Give to everyone who asks you, and if anyone takes what belongs to you, do not demand it back.* [31] *Do to others as you would have them do to you.*

[32] *"If you love those who love you, what credit is that to you? Even sinners love those who love them.* [33] *And if you do good to those who are good to you, what credit is that to you? Even sinners do that.* [34] *And if you lend to those from whom you expect repayment, what credit is that to you? Even sinners lend to sinners, expecting to be repaid in full.* [35] *But love your enemies, do good to them, and lend to them without expecting to get anything back. Then your reward will be great, and you will be children of the Most High, because he is kind to the ungrateful and wicked.* [36] *Be merciful, just as your Father is merciful.* [37] *"Do not judge, and you will not be judged. Do not condemn, and you will not be condemned. Forgive, and you will be forgiven*

ON THE ILLUSION OF GUILT AND FULFILLING OUR PURPOSE

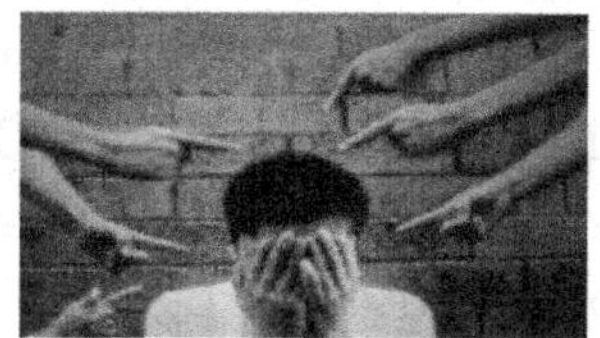

Once upon a time in a land not far from yours
there was a girl and her father:

"Father, I'm starting to think that guilt may be
an illusion." The daughter stated. "You may be
onto something." The father responded.

Guilt is a feeling of reflection on the past. Guilt is not present.
Guilt is remembered; it's processed. Guilt is not based on
something that is happening, but rather is based on something
that has "happened". When we go back to guilt, we revert
to memory, and memory is past. More and more people are
starting to realize that the past doesn't exist. The past is no
longer here. The past has already happened, it has no place
with us now in our present existence. Guilt holds us back
and prevents us from becoming all that we can be. Guilt
prevents us from becoming the person that we should be.
We should not allow past guilt to take away our present lives
from us. We should not "feel" guilt from our past, and instead
focus on our present lives; we should focus on today.

When I say not to feel guilty and focus on today, I don't mean
for us to lose our conscience and become these people who
go out and do anything and not feel any remorse. Rather, if
the guilt is holding us back from our true purpose and from
fulfilling the things that God wants us to do and reach, then
we shouldn't allow guilt to take a residence inside of us.

We can't let guilt have a place in our lives. In order for us
to focus on guilt, we would have to focus on the past. We
shouldn't dig up these old skeletons and hold onto them and
let them weigh us down; preventing us from being closer
to God and his purpose for us and those around us.

Guilt is like a disease that slowly kills, and we shouldn't allow guilt to kill us. Guilt has no place in our lives; guilt is disease; guilt is a hindrance.

But if we choose to focus on today, and remain in the present, then it is impossible to focus on the past, which makes it impossible for guilt to have a place in our lives. Instead we should focus on today and what we are doing right now, and also on how the actions that we are performing right now, will ultimately fulfill our purpose, and bring us closer to God.

I believe that guilt is a trick of the enemy. Guilt is the Devil's trick to hold us back and make us feel like we are unworthy to be with God, when God already loves us, and has already chosen us. As I heard a preacher once say, *God knew everything you were going to do before you even did it!* So, your sins and offenses are not going to prevent Him from continuing to love you, nor will they make you unworthy of His Love. When we begin to feel the first feelings of guilt try to come upon us, the first thing we must do is ask for forgiveness, and then LET IT GO!

We can't remain focused on it. We must ask forgiveness from God for whatever sin that we've committed which is weighing us down, and also apologize and ask forgiveness of whatever person (if there is one) that was involved in or hurt by our offense. Once we've done this, we must let it go and continue to live in the present. Because guilt is based on actions in the past, and past does not exist, then this means that guilt is not real! Guilt is a façade, it is an illusion, it's a trick that prevents us from being closer to God and fulfilling our purpose.

So, in order to protect ourselves from the trap and trick of guilt, we must stay in the present, live for today, live with God today, and live freely today.

Only the present is real.

<u>Hebrews 10:21-22</u>

New Living Translation (NLT)

21 And since we have a great High Priest who rules over God's house, 22 let us go right into the presence of God with sincere hearts fully trusting him. For our guilty consciences have been sprinkled with Christ's blood to make us clean, and our bodies have been washed with pure water.

RENEWING OUR MINDS DAILY

Once upon a time in a land not far from yours,
there was a girl and her father:

"Father, why does it sometimes feel that God has
forsaken me?" the daughter asked. "Well, during those
times, have you ever thought that maybe you have
forsaken God?" the father asked in return.

Have you ever had those days or weeks, where you felt like
nothing in the world could hold you down? Where you felt
like no matter where you went, you could physically feel God
right there beside you? And conversely, have you ever had
those days or weeks, where God couldn't feel further away?

I've noticed that during the times that God seems far away,
it's usually because we have forgotten to renew our minds
daily. Just believing in God every day, isn't enough to keep us
fortified spiritually every day. We have to use our resources.
We must go back to the basics and read our bibles, even if it
is only a scripture per day. We need to pray, even if it is only a
couple of minutes in the morning, thanking God for waking us
up, and asking Him to keep us protected throughout the day.
Even putting on your favorite televangelist or some recordings
from spiritual gurus in your car during your commute, will
help to put you in the "right" frame of mind for the day.

I've realized that including God in your life daily through
some activity, does wonders for keeping your mind renewed.
These small daily actions fortify our spirit, and help us to
always "feel" that God is with us all day, every day.

Romans 12:2

New International Version (NIV)

*2 Do not conform to the pattern of this world, but be transformed
by the renewing of your mind. Then you will be able to test and*

approve what God's will is—his good, pleasing and perfect will.

Ephesians 4:22-24

Amplified Bible (AMP)

22 Strip yourselves of your former nature [put off and discard your old unrenewed self] which characterized your previous manner of life and becomes corrupt through lusts and desires that spring from delusion; 23 And be constantly renewed in the spirit of your mind [having a fresh mental and spiritual attitude], 24 And put on the new nature (the regenerate self) created in God's image, [Godlike] in true righteousness and holiness.

SAVE YOURSELF

Once upon a time, in a land not far from yours,
there was a girl and her father:

"Father, what is the most important thing a leader can do?" The girl asked. "Set an honest example." The father answered.

Saving yourself is an important concept to internalize as a Christian. At the moment of our salvation when we decide to come to God, we realize then how important it is to save ourselves by saving our souls. But as time progresses, we forget. We forget that in order to stay close to God, and in order to continue to walk in peace with Him, we must first save ourselves.

a life that goes with it. If you are truly called by
God to lead, he will give you not only the Grace,
but the Strength to live this kind of life.

Now some might think that this sounds harsh or even unreasonable, but let's consider the opposite for a moment. What do people tend to think when they see Christian leaders being hauled away on criminal and sexual charges? And how do these charges reflect, not only on them, but on Christianity as a whole? It makes Christians and Christianity seem like a joke, and it gives satan and things which are evil the glory. Not only that, but the results of a great Christian leader's fall, are the many Christian Causalities in the form of the souls that followed them.

So, before you decide to stand up in front of God's
people as a leader and representative, search yourself,
monitor your behavior and "truly" seek the Lord about
it. **Leading is not a privilege, but a responsibility.**

<u>Leadership is not about being before people,
it's about living before God.</u>

Most of the time, when we are new to a church or an organization, we are eager to help and, in some cases, take a leadership role. While this is an excellent aspiration to have, it is important not to act "prematurely" on it. Before we become leaders, we must know how to follow. And when I say follow, I am not referring to "Holy men" but to **God**. Unless we have learned to follow God completely and wholly, (while denying our fleshly impulses), **we shouldn't be before God's people as a leader**. In this instance it is best to sit down, be taught, have patience, learn who our new selves are in God and then go forth from there.

The reason why I suggest this, is when we come before God's people as leaders, we need to keep in mind and recognize that we are God's representatives here on earth. When you lead God's people you must have His spirit working inside of you, which means: <u>you are called to a higher standard.</u>

When you are before God's people there are no more excuses such as: "I'm Only Human" or "We All Make Mistakes". If you feel that you have really been called by God to serve His people, make sure that you are willing to live

<u>1 Timothy 4:16</u>

New Living Translation (NLT)

16 Keep a close watch on how you live and on your teaching. Stay true to what is right for the sake of your own salvation and the salvation of those who hear you.

<u>Titus 2:7-8</u>

New Living Translation (NLT)

7 And you yourself must be an example to them by doing good works of every kind. Let everything you do reflect the integrity and seriousness of your teaching. 8 Teach the truth so that

your teaching can't be criticized. Then those who oppose us will be ashamed and have nothing bad to say about us.

<u>Matthew 6:1-4</u>

New Living Translation (NLT)

"Watch out! Don't do your good deeds publicly, to be admired by others, for you will lose the reward from your Father in heaven. 2 When you give to someone in need, don't do as the hypocrites do—blowing trumpets in the synagogues and streets to call attention to their acts of charity! I tell you the truth, they have received all the reward they will ever get. 3 But when you give to someone in need, don't let your left hand know what your right hand is doing. 4 Give your gifts in private, and your Father, who sees everything, will reward you.

THE TRUE COST OF
SIN IS OUR PEACE

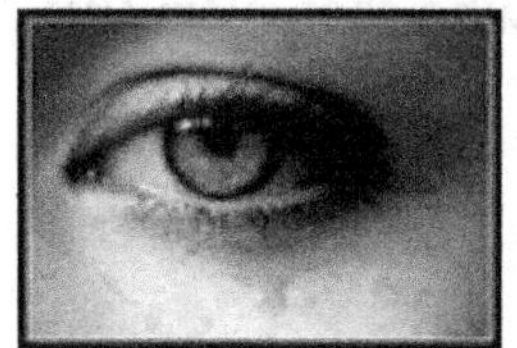

Once upon a time, in a land not far from yours,
there was a girl and her father:

"Father, what are the consequences of sin?" the girl asked. "There are many, but mainly not being able to enter into the Kingdom of Heaven and live with God." The father answered. "What do you mean by many?" the girl asked. "Sin will steal your Peace, and once your Peace is gone you self-destruct and begin to destroy everything that's beautiful about you." The father answered.

As Christians one of the primary focuses of our Faith is abstaining from sin, with the main objective of avoiding hell and God's wrath and disappointment; hereby ensuring our way into heaven. But I think the reason why some Christians sin so much and abuse God's grace is because, heaven seems far away. It isn't imminent or in the immediate future, so this makes it easy to sin today, and deal with repentance tomorrow. But what is the true cost of our sin? Is it the revocation of our admittance to heaven, and the erasure of our name in the book of life? Or is the real cost of sin more immediate than we think?

We always talk about abstaining from sin, but
what behaviors constitute as sin?

Galatians 5 names a few:

Galatians 5:19-21

King James Version (KJV)

*¹⁹ Now the works of the flesh are manifest, which are these;
Adultery, fornication, uncleanness, lasciviousness,*

*²⁰ Idolatry, witchcraft, hatred, variance, emulations,
wrath, strife, seditions, heresies,*

*²¹ Envyings, murders, drunkenness, revellings, and such like: of the
which I tell you before, as I have also told you in time past, that*

they which do such things shall not inherit the kingdom of God.

And these sins are defined more simply in
the New Living Translation as:

[19] *When you follow the desires of your sinful nature, the results are very clear: sexual immorality, impurity, lustful pleasures,* [20] *idolatry, sorcery, hostility, quarreling, jealousy, outbursts of anger, selfish ambition, dissension, division,* [21] *envy, drunkenness, wild parties, and other sins like these. Let me tell you again, as I have before, that anyone living that sort of life will not inherit the Kingdom of God.*

Yes. All these behaviors are bad; and yes, if we continue to perform these behaviors when we are aware that we shouldn't, we will not inherit the Kingdom of God. But... there is also another thing we lose out on when we continue to sin: Peace.

I truly believe that God gave us these commandments and warned us not to sin for our own benefit here on Earth. For example: Fornication and Adultery comes at a high price. Yes, you will get that momentary fleshly and/or emotional satisfaction that you are looking for, but at what cost? Fornication and Adultery can end up leading to unwanted pregnancies, broken hearts and relationships, negative sad and depressing emotions, broken families, lost marriages and innocent people as collateral damage; just to name a few. Who would want to suffer these things just to satisfy some fleshly urge; and on top of that risk going to hell?

Another set of sins: *Hostility, quarreling, jealousy, outbursts of anger, selfish ambition, dissension, division,* [21] *envy, drunkenness, wild parties, and other sins like these.* These sins will leave you tired, stressed out, looking much older than your actual age, and lead you to do things that you will regret and suffer immediate consequences for. All these sins are "totally" avoidable if we are really living in Christ and walking in Faith. The stress and negative immediate consequences

that these sinful actions bring, just **are not** worth losing
our peace over, or our future heavenly lives with God.

Let's be bigger and better Christians. Let's represent God to the
fullest and also enjoy His Peace and blessings here on Earth as
we are living. Let's allow our lives and our existence to be bigger
than ourselves and our fleshly desires. Let's not let the devil
and these same fleshly desires steal our Peace and our Joy.

Sinful Satisfaction just isn't worth it. But a life with God is.

<u>Galatians 5:22-25</u>

New Living Translation (NLT)

[22] *But the Holy Spirit produces this kind of fruit in our lives: love, joy, peace, patience, kindness, goodness, faithfulness,* [23] *gentleness, and self-control. There is no law against these things!*

[24] *Those who belong to Christ Jesus have nailed the passions and desires of their sinful nature to his cross and crucified them there.* [25] *Since we are living by the Spirit, let us follow the Spirit's leading in every part of our lives.*

WHICH IS STRONGER... GOOD OR EVIL?

Once upon a time in a land not far from yours,
there was a girl and her father:

"Father, which is stronger, good or evil?" the daughter asked.
"Hmm…that's a good question." The father replied.

I have often pondered this question and have tried to come up with an unbiased answer. I've tried to come up with an answer that truly is, and that is not purely what I want it to be. To start, we all know that both are very powerful, and always at war with one another. Battle after battle tends to be won one way or the other, but neither has won the war. I believe that proof of this is evident in all of us.

We have times where we let good be in control of us, and base all of our decisions on goodness. When we are walking with Good we feel lightness of spirit, and powerful in an open and all-encompassing way. We feel that nothing can truly harm us because our goodness keeps us safe.

On the other hand, there is evil. There are times that we walk with evil, in denial about it or not. We indulge in selfish pleasures, exact our revenge, and feel untouchable in the power which evil gives us. We walk around self-assured and self-reliant needing no one, and not letting anyone get in our way "or else".

We have all experienced the power that good and evil yields to us and have decided which power we like the taste of better. Some of us prefer good and others evil. This is what makes the world such a colorful place; the different mixtures of good and evil. But at the end of the day, the question still is: which is stronger?

<u>The answer that I'm leaning towards:</u>

That good and evil are both equal parts of the same whole. What makes one stronger than the other depends on the person wielding its power.

There has been evidence of this all throughout history, from eastern philosophy all the way to popular culture and Harry Potter!

This is why I believe that it is so important for us to continue trusting in God and loving the people around us. We can tip the scales in the war of good and evil in Good's favor if we keep Trusting in God and help others to Trust in Him also. If we can get more people to stand together and wield the power of Good instead of evil, I truly believe that we can finally win the war. And finally, in the end Good will stand victorious.

Proverbs 14:22

New International Version (NIV)

22 Do not those who plot evil go astray? But those who plan what is good find love and faithfulness.

Luke 6:44-45

New International Version (NIV)

44 Each tree is recognized by its own fruit. People do not pick figs from thornbushes, or grapes from briers. 45 A good man brings good things out of the good stored up in his heart, and an evil man brings evil things out of the evil stored up in his heart. For the mouth speaks what the heart is full of.

1 Peter 3:10-11

New International Version (NIV)

10 For, "Whoever would love life and see good days must keep their tongue from evil and their lips from deceitful speech. 11 They must turn from evil and do good; they must seek peace and pursue it.

WHY DO CHRISTIANS SIN?

Once upon a time, in a land not far from yours
there was a girl and her father.

"Father, why do Christians sin?" the girl asked. "Because it is in our nature and because we are tempted. This is why we must walk in the spirit." He answered. "But dad, could it also be that maybe some Christians don't really see Heaven or Hell as being real?" The girl asked. "I don't know daughter, maybe?" He answered.

In the bible there are many answers for why Christians sin: the flesh, temptation, spiritual and personal weakness just to name a few. But have you ever really sat down and asked yourself either one of these two questions: Why do I sin? (and/or) Why don't I sin?

Maybe the reason Christians sin, and then do so again, even after repentance, is because Heaven or Hell isn't real to them. It can't be. If the Christian sinner really considered Hell to be a real and actual place, why take the risk in going there? There can be nothing in this world; no feeling, no person, or any situation that would be worth the risk of going to Hell. And not only that, but why would a Christian risk offending God and betraying his love? Which opens another can of worms: does the Christian sinner truly believe there is a God?

I think Paul says it best in his letter to the Romans 8:37-39 *For I am convinced that neither death nor life, neither angels nor demons, neither the present nor the future, nor any powers, neither height nor depth, nor anything else in all creation, will be able to separate us from the love of God that is in Christ Jesus our Lord.*

I am truly asking this question not in judgment, but in spiritual

Christian curiosity. If I love God, and know that if I break his commandments and sin against His love that I am putting myself at risk for Hell, why would I want to do that, logically? I wouldn't want to, right? So what part of our Christianity, of our faith and beliefs do we have to turn off, to be able to give in to our nature, to our sins? Is this where the forgiveness factor comes in? Does the forgiveness make sin okay?

I guess an example of sin against love can be taken personally. If you have a person that loves you to death, that loves you unconditionally, someone that you know will forgive you for anything; do you take advantage of that? And if you do, what would be the consequence of this? Would their love for you be the same, would their forgiveness unceasingly continue?

Yes, I know that it's hard to compare a human's forgiveness to God's, but does not the bible say that we were made in God's own image? Now considering God doesn't have a flesh and blood body, we can only assume that God made us in his own image internally. And if internally, we have a limit for forgiveness, does this mean that God does also? And furthermore, how do we really know that we have been truly forgiven by God after our trespasses? Are we forgiven by Faith? And, if we believe to be forgiven by Faith, then why don't we deny sin by this same Faith?

In the bible is says that blasphemy is the only unforgiveable sin. Many Christians don't believe that they have ever found themselves guilty of blasphemy but, is not sin itself a form of blasphemy?

Blasphemy is defined as: *the __act__ of insulting or showing contempt or lack of reverence for God.* (Merriam Webster dictionary).

Blasphemy is also defined as: *the __act__ or offense of speaking sacrilegiously about God or sacred things* (oxford dictionary).

Most Christians believe that the only form of blasphemy is that of *speaking* sacrilegiously against God, but blasphemy is not limited to just words, blasphemy can also include acts. So, then the question is: what is a sacrilegious act?

Sacrilege is defined as: *violation or misuse of what is regarded as sacred* (oxford dictionary).

Now I ask, what is it which we regard to be the most sacred in our religion? <u>God's Love</u>. So, when we violate this love in the form of sinful behavior, is that not blasphemous? And if we are committing blasphemy then according to scripture we are not forgiven.

At what point will we stop taking advantage of God's Love and realize that Heaven and Hell are real places? When we were saved we were saved from sin. Why then do we go act like dogs; vomiting up the bad and going back to eat it?

If we have chosen to be Christians, using our own free will, when will we start behaving like Christians? **<u>It is not ok to sin</u>**. We have been called to a higher purpose, and with that calling we were given power by the Holy Spirit. Each time we sin, we blaspheme against that same Holy Spirit which was given to us. Why risk unforgiveness and "eternal consequences" for momentary satisfaction?

So, I ask the question again: Why do Christians sin?

<u>Answer:</u> The only place where these answers can originate is within the person asking themselves and God.

<u>Mark 3:29</u>

New Living Translation (NLT)

²⁹ *but anyone who blasphemes the Holy Spirit will never be forgiven. This is a sin with eternal consequences."*

2 Peter 2:19-22
New Living Translation (NLT)

<u>For you are a slave to whatever controls you</u>. ²⁰ *And when people escape from the wickedness of the world by knowing our Lord and Savior Jesus Christ and then get tangled up and enslaved by sin again, they are worse off than before.* ²¹ *It would be better if they had never known the way to righteousness than to know it and then reject the command they were given to live a holy life.* ²² *They prove the truth of this proverb: "A dog returns to its vomit." And another says, "A washed pig returns to the mud."*

WHY THE BAD DAYS?

Once upon a time in a land not far from yours,
there was a girl and her father:

"Father, I don't understand. I've been doing everything that
God has been telling me to do, and I'm still having bad days!
Why?" the girl asked. "Every day that we live, we live it for a
reason, and for a purpose. If you are having bad days, it is not
a punishment, there is a bigger reason. It is all a part of God's
plan for you. Don't worry daughter. God will reveal His plan
for you, and the reasons for all your bad days in due time. In
the meantime, just continue to live." The father answered.

Why do we have "the bad days"? As Christians, one of
the first concepts we learn is that if we do good things,
then good things will happen for us. Following this logic,
as Christians who are constantly doing good things, we
should *only* have good things coming to us in return.
Given this, we should never be subject to bad days, yet we
are. So, I ask the question again, why the bad days?

I've heard the cliché answer of, "*So we can learn to lean on
God*". And my question in return is, "*Is that it?*" There has to be
more to suffering through a horrible day and/or horrible days,
than just learning to lean on God? There are so many other
situations where we can learn to lean on God that doesn't involve
physical, mental and emotional acute pain. I'm not saying that
learning to lean on God during the bad days is a bad thing;
I'm just thinking that there must be more to it than that.

My current theory: In some way, this bad day holds a necessary
experience or lesson essential to my growth as a Christian.

They say that when you experience something personally,
that you are learning it the "hard way". I've noticed that
when we learn things the hard way, these lessons are
the ones we remember the most. These "hard-learned"

lessons, stick with us longer than the ones which we learn vicariously through the experiences of others.

In James 1:2-4 it says, *Dear brothers and sisters, when troubles come your way, consider it an opportunity for great joy. For you know that when your faith is tested, your endurance has a chance to grow. So let it grow, for when your endurance is fully developed, you will be perfect and complete, needing nothing.*

When I stumbled upon this scripture it really got me thinking. Is James trying to say that the reason for the bad days and the trials, is for us to become *"perfect and complete, needing nothing"*? Now that is true peace isn't? This "needing nothing"! Oh, how this is truly ministering to the soul. To be in a state of "no need", is to be spiritually free, and not dependent on anything in this Earth. We can be *"perfect and complete"* in our Faith in God. This almost seems to be the pinnacle of "Christian" Self-Actualization. This one scripture seems to try to give our bad days, trials and tribulations some kind of bigger meaning doesn't it?

I guess this is why it is so important for us to pick-up our bibles every now and then and look for some answers to our personal questions ourselves. I can't say that in the midst of all my bad days that this scripture provides mental clarity for me during my moments of despair, but at the end of them, it's good to know that all of the bad days recently suffered weren't *entirely* for nothing. That God really does have a plan at work in the times when life seems to be so pointless. We have to remember to have Faith, and not to let despair continue to hold us in its bosom.

YOUR JOY IS "YOUR" JOY

Once upon a time in a land not far from yours,
there was a girl and her father.

"Father, I think I'm starting to discover the things that actually create and destroy our joy." The daughter stated. "And what is that?" the Father asked. "Perspective." The daughter answered.

I'm starting to realize that the creator and destroyer of joy is "we" ourselves. We can choose to hold onto our joy or give into to doubt and despair. I know this concept at first glance may sound simple, but I think we all know enough to know, that it is not that way. When we logically look at something it makes sense, but logic and feelings are two different things. We may "know" that we should always feel joy when walking with God, but we "feel" joyless at times during our walk with Him.

Often people will blame the devil, other people and outer circumstances as disturbances and thieves of their joy, but that's impossible. Joy is perspective, and when things happen to us we tend to lose that joyful perspective. Life looks gray, hopeless and pointless; instead of bright, hopeful and full of possibility. Often, circumstances influence our perspective, and even though we know better, sometimes our emotional perspectives cloud our spiritual judgment, reasoning and beliefs.

I have yet to discover what the cure for constantly keeping our joy is, but I am glad that at least I'm starting to understand the root of the problem. I am grateful that I am now able to at least diagnose the disease that plagues me. You might wonder why I constantly write about Hope and Faith. It's is not because I am an authority on it. But it is because I believe that these are the areas in which all cures lie.

I believe…therefore I am hopeful and have Faith even if sometimes my emotional perspectives try to tell me otherwise. I believe in the light at the end of the tunnel. I believe that the keys to our human happiness lie in joy, and that joy will ultimately lead us and keep us close to God.

Your joy is yours. Don't allow yourself to take that away from you.

Psalm 94:18-20

New International Version (NIV)

18 When I said, "My foot is slipping," your unfailing love, Lord, supported me. 19 When anxiety was great within me, your consolation brought me joy.

James 1:2-4

New International Version (NIV)

*2 **Consider it pure joy**, my brothers and sisters, whenever you face trials of many kinds, 3 because you know that the testing of your faith produces perseverance. 4 Let perseverance finish its work so that you may be mature and complete, not lacking anything.*

IS MY LIVING IN VAIN?

When I was a child, my mother sang in a small group composed of 4 women at our church. They would sing the most harmonious melodies, and you would never think that so much good sound could come from just four people. There was on song in particular by The Clark Sisters, for which they were locally renowned entitled "Is My Living In Vain."

This song was something of a dialogue between a Christian and God. The Christian is asking God if all their sacrifices of the flesh and righteous way of living means anything; if everything they have sacrificed for God will eventually be rewarded, and if it counts or matters at all?

I honestly believe that at some point in our long-term relationship with God, we start to wonder is my living in vain? Sometimes we can't help but notice people with whom we are familiar, behaving and acting in ways which are sinful and go against God's word. According to the bible these people which sin and know better, and which don't behave in a Godly manner, are living outside the will of God and are supposed to be punished; not blessed. Conversely, those of us who live Godly, keep God's commandments and live by his word, are supposed to be blessed and exalted.

The reason why the song I mentioned earlier comes to mind is because at some point in our Christian walk, we may experience the opposite of what I just stated. Sometimes we see the sinner exalted, and the Christian struggle. At times, it seems as if the sinner is constantly bestowed blessing after blessing, and reward after reward, as we suffer and struggle with difficulty even though we are living Godly. We watch as the sinner enjoys new cars, good relationships, promotions and joy; while we may struggle to pay bills, find "the one", maintain (or find) jobs and stay in good spirits.

When we are presented with these situations, we can't help but ask God, "is my living in vain?" Does my Christian life matter? Why am I, in my goodness and holiness suffering so badly? When will you bless me?

Will you bless me?

Sometimes I wonder when we encounter situations such as these in our Christian walk, if it is a test. Is God testing our Faith in Him, and the promises he made to us in His word? Will we cling to him even stronger, or will we break down and revert to sinful ways when it seems our Christian living is a waste? Or is time the illusion here?

As long as we are living for God, our blessings "have" to come. Our blessings are on their way. Our living is not in vain. Maybe the sinner's punishment hasn't caught up with them yet, just like maybe our blessing hasn't caught up with us yet. I've heard a preacher say that a blessing delayed is not a blessing denied, and it seems that the harder it gets to believe, the more imperative it is that we do so.

We are supposed to serve God because He is God and we love him for that and that alone. As Christians, I think we can sometimes put too much emphasis on blessings and things we want and desire, that we forget that these things are not our sole motivation for serving God. Allow the sinner to be as they are and let us take our focus away from them.

Let us believe.

Let us find peace and rest in our difficult situations; let us believe as we never have before. Let us know *that we know, that we know*, that our living is not in vain; whether the "physical" blessings come or not. Let us put the blinders on and focus solely on our own relationship with God. We do not only serve God only because we want to be blessed. We serve Him because we choose to, and because He loves us.

So, when you find yourself asking: "Is My Living In Vain?" Talk to yourself and say, *"No, Of course not! It's not all in vain."*

Psalm 73:1-26
New Living Translation (NLT)

1 Truly God is good to Israel,
to those whose hearts are pure.
2 But as for me, I almost lost my footing.
My feet were slipping, and I was almost gone.
3 For I envied the proud
when I saw them prosper despite their wickedness.
4 They seem to live such painless lives;
their bodies are so healthy and strong.
5 They don't have troubles like other people;
they're not plagued with problems like everyone else.
6 They wear pride like a jeweled necklace
and clothe themselves with cruelty.
7 These fat cats have everything
their hearts could ever wish for!
8 They scoff and speak only evil;
in their pride they seek to crush others.
9 They boast against the very heavens,
and their words strut throughout the earth.
10 And so the people are dismayed and confused,
drinking in all their words.
11 "What does God know?" they ask.

"Does the Most High even know what's happening?"
12 Look at these wicked people—
enjoying a life of ease while their riches multiply.
13 Did I keep my heart pure for nothing?
Did I keep myself innocent for no reason?
14 I get nothing but trouble all day long;
every morning brings me pain.

15 If I had really spoken this way to others,
I would have been a traitor to your people.
16 So I tried to understand why the wicked prosper.
But what a difficult task it is!
17 Then I went into your sanctuary, O God,
and I finally understood the destiny of the wicked.
18 Truly, you put them on a slippery path
and send them sliding over the cliff to destruction.
19 In an instant they are destroyed,
completely swept away by terrors.
20 When you arise, O Lord,
you will laugh at their silly ideas
as a person laughs at dreams in the morning.

21 Then I realized that my heart was bitter,
and I was all torn up inside.
22 I was so foolish and ignorant—
I must have seemed like a senseless animal to you.
23 Yet I still belong to you;
you hold my right hand.
24 You guide me with your counsel,
leading me to a glorious destiny.
25 Whom have I in heaven but you?
I desire you more than anything on earth.

26 My health may fail, and my spirit may grow weak,
but God remains the strength of my heart;
he is mine forever.

1 Corinthians 15:58

English Standard Version (ESV)

58 Therefore, my beloved brothers, be steadfast,
immovable, always abounding in the work of the Lord,
knowing that in the Lord your labor is not in vain.

DON'T REPRESS YOUR POTENTIAL

I apologize in advance for the technical tone of this reading, but there was just no way of getting around the technical parts to explain the amazing mystery hidden within.

While reading a medical science book, I came across something profound. The book stated that *"because all cells found in the body are derived from the fertilized ova, all cells have the potential to perform '**all**' body functions."* The text went further to state, *"as cells differentiate, <u>this potential is repressed,</u> and the mature cell is capable of performing only specific functions."*

So, put simply, we all are derived from a single cell (a combo of mother's egg and father's sperm). Even though we all start from this single *unspecialized* cell, we soon develop *specialized* cells like brain cells, heart cells, skin cells, etcetera. Given this information, the passage is stating that all of our newly developed cells have the potential to perform in a variety of functions, but as they mature (grow and age) they lose this potential and can only perform in a "limited" function.

When I read this passage it blew my mind. All I could think after reading this was, "if this change takes place in us on a "cellular" level, is it no wonder that this same change takes place in us on an all-encompassing mental, spiritual, and emotional level?"

Haven't you noticed that as you have aged, the things which you once dreamed about seem to become less possible or less likely to happen? Have you seen your dreams as a child go from: "I wish I could fly" to the dreams of your teenage years being: "I wish I could drive."

When did we stop believing in the great potential of possibility in everything our hearts could once conceive, to the limited goals and functions of everyday life?

When did the units of our existence that once held so much potential and possibility become "specialized" or in other words, *limited*?

Let us encourage each other and remind ourselves that we are limitless beings, and that God created us this way from birth. Do not let "maturity" take your dreams away from you. Do not forget that if one of the smallest parts of you has the potential to be anything that it wants, why wouldn't the great "whole" of you, not be able to do the exact same thing?

2 Corinthians 4:7-10

New Living Translation (NLT)

7 We now have this light shining in our hearts, but we ourselves are like fragile clay jars containing this great treasure. This makes it clear that our great power is from God, not from ourselves.

8 We are pressed on every side by troubles, but we are not crushed. We are perplexed, but not driven to despair. 9 We are hunted down, but never abandoned by God. We get knocked down, but we are not destroyed. 10 Through suffering, our bodies continue to share in the death of Jesus so that the life of Jesus may also be seen in our bodies.

Don't repress your light.

Don't repress your potential.

HOLDING ONTO HOPE…GOD'S WORKING BEHIND THE SCENES

Once upon a time, in a land not far from yours,
there was a girl and her father:

"Father, why does it seem as if God is not answering
my prayers?" the girl asked. "But he is. Just keep your
Faith. You may not see it, but God is working behind
the scenes in your favor." The father answered.

Have you ever been in or confronted with a seemingly hopeless
situation? Have you ever felt like no matter how hard you
prayed, that you couldn't get a prayer through to God's ears?

If you have, don't be hard on yourself or God. At some point we
have all been there in our Christian walk with God. I believe
the reason why there are so many faith scriptures in the bible
is because God knows that our human side is prone to doubt.

I just want to encourage those of you going through a rough
patch right now, to not give up on God. Just because we can't
see things changing before our eyes doesn't mean that God
is not working on it. Faith is the cornerstone of our walk and
belief in God and it is important to rely on this same Faith
in the hard times; especially when we feel as if we can't see
a way out of our current negative situation or dilemma.

Here are a few scriptures to help us hold onto to our
unyielding Faith in God during these times.

Hebrews 11:1-3

New Living Translation (NLT)

Great Examples of Faith

*11 Faith is the confidence that what we hope for will actually
happen; it gives us assurance about things we cannot see. ² Through*

their faith, the people in days of old earned a good reputation.

[3] By faith we understand that the entire universe was formed at God's command, that what we now see did not come from anything that can be seen.

Luke 18:41-43

New Living Translation (NLT)

[41] "What do you want me to do for you?"

"Lord," he said, "I want to see!"

[42] And Jesus said, "All right, receive your sight! Your faith has healed you." [43] Instantly the man could see, and he followed Jesus, praising God. And all who saw it praised God, too.

1 Timothy 1:19

New Living Translation (NLT)

[19] Cling to your faith in Christ, and keep your conscience clear. For some people have deliberately violated their consciences; as a result, their faith has been shipwrecked.

Proverbs 23:17-19

New International Version (NIV)

17 Do not let your heart envy sinners, but always be zealous for the fear of the Lord. [18] There is surely a future hope for you, and your hope will not be cut off.

Romans 5:3-4

New International Version (NIV)

3 Not only so, but we also glory in our sufferings, because we know that suffering produces perseverance; 4 perseverance, character; and character, hope.

FAITH AS WE WERE TAUGHT IT, AND FAITH AS WE KNOW IT

Faith as we were taught it and Faith as we know it, can be two totally different sets of knowledge and experience all concerning the same Faith. There is a Faith that was taught to us by parents, grandparents and friends, and then there is a Faith that, if we are willing, we learn ourselves. There comes a point in our walk with Christ, (especially if our walk started in early childhood) where we begin to realize that "mommy's" Faith or "daddy's" Faith, is not _our_ Faith.

I believe that initially this may make us feel guilty or lost, but it is really the beginning of a wonderful journey in which we get to know God for ourselves. When we start to know God for ourselves (outside of the terms in which we were taught), is when I truly believe we start to become Christians in truth. Maybe a "taught" Faith is enough to sustain us at first (just like mother's milk), but as we grow in Faith we require different and stronger nourishment if we are to continue to grow. I also believe, that this more mature level of growth can only come through personal experience, and the willingness and strength to venture out on our own and find Christ for ourselves.

For instance, growing up, the Christ I was taught was harsh, but fair. He was also presented to me as this one-dimensional being who was quick to punish, and slow to forgive. For a very long time, I was the same way. I was hard on myself and others, and was very slow to forgive them (and even myself), if a mistake was made. But, as I began to grow and learn Christ for myself, I realized that there was more than just that one dimension to Him (and also to myself). Once I started to read for myself and think for myself where my Faith was concerned, I was able evolve. I stopped being so angry and began to seek the truth for myself. It was once I was able to find Christ for myself, that I was able to let go of resentment and breathe for the first time in my saved life. How many of you are still suffering under the weight of Faith as you were taught it, and suffering from the pain of someone else's Jesus Christ?

Don't be afraid to find and define God based on your own research, study and experience. Once you are able to personalize your experience with Christ, then you will be able to walk in the fullness of what it means to be a Christian. You will be able to walk in the fullness of Love.

<u>1 Corinthians 13:11-13</u>

New Life Version (NLV)

11 When I was a child, I spoke like a child. I thought like a child. I understood like a child. Now I am a man. I do not act like a child anymore. 12 Now that which we see is as if we were looking in a broken mirror. But then we will see everything. Now I know only a part. But then I will know everything in a perfect way. That is how God knows me right now. 13 And now we have these three: faith and hope and love, but the greatest of these is love.

WHAT WE ARE TRULY LOOKING FOR

God's love is so *complete*. Try as we might to replicate it, we never will. There's no worry that we can't trust Him, no worry that He will ever leave us, no worry that He won't always be there, and conversely the assurance that He always has been.

I believe that the point that we are all trying to reach as Christians is not to be "Christian", but to continually feel and be that *complete* Love that God is. When we walk *with* that *complete* love ingrained into every fiber of our being every day, we can't help but radiate holiness, forgiveness, non-judgment, acceptance, peace, joy and a oneness with everything and everyone. When we walk *with* this *complete* love ingrained into every fiber of our being, sin is not even a temptation, it doesn't even register.

I believe that we are able to feel bits and pieces of this *complete* love in the form of human to human contact because we were all created in God's image. So, it is within our human to human contacts that we feel and sense pieces of this *complete* love. We feel it when we look at our children, we feel it when we can be ourselves with trusted friends, when we are comforted by a love one and when we are alone with the person we love most on this Earth. While at times these "feelings" can be fleeting and maybe even change in some way over time, the residual of these moments of *complete* love, stay with us and sustain us, and at times feel more real to us than anything we have ever known. Even though we can't touch this love or see it, it's so real, it's so *complete*, it's so God.

I believe that the key to really internalizing these spiritual beliefs and values is truly so simple and yet at times can be most complex; the key is to *Love*. The key is to always try to walk with this *complete* Love ingrained into every fiber of our being, in every situation, thought and action every day in every way. If we can accomplish this, then we can transcend to a higher plane; one where we are ever closer to God throughout this existence until that day when we are taken back to be at peace with Him in that ever great and *complete* Love. When we are looking for Love (whether romantic or platonic), what it is that we are truly looking for...is God.

Deuteronomy 7:9

New Living Translation (NLT)

9 Understand, therefore, that the Lord your God is indeed God. He is the faithful God who keeps his covenant for a thousand generations and lavishes his unfailing love on those who love him and obey his commands.

Ephesians 3:17-19

New Living Translation (NLT)

17 Then Christ will make his home in your hearts as you trust in him. Your roots will grow down into God's love and keep you strong. 18 And may you have the power to understand, as all God's people should, how wide, how long, how high, and how deep his love is. 19 May you experience the love of Christ, though it is too great to understand fully. Then you will be made <u>complete</u> with all the fullness of life and power that comes from God.

1 John 2:5

New Living Translation (NLT)

*5 But those who obey God's word truly show how <u>completely</u> they love him. **That is how we know we are living in him.***

TRUE LOVE MAKES US INCAPABLE OF SIN

If you have a significant other, someone you truly love, like a wife, husband, boyfriend, girlfriend, or even a love interest; think about how you feel about them. When you are in deep love with this person, no other person exists for you, let alone the thought of being with someone else, or cheating on the person you love so much. There are many reasons why you don't want to hurt them or sin against the love which you have together. For one, other people don't even register on your romantic radar. You could be in a room full of beautiful people and the only thing that you are wishing for while you are there, is the person you love most. You wouldn't do anything that could possibly damage the love that you share, and the joy that their love gives you.

Now I'm not trying to say that we sin because we have no Love for God, rather I am saying that we haven't learned *how* to Love God. We've learned how to fear Him, respect Him, and try to trade good behavior for things that we want from Him. The bible teaches us that God is our father, and we, in our human minds, limit our relationship with Him to that of a parent. How limited we can be in our thinking and our love towards God. God is all Love, not just parental Love.

I wonder how our relationship with God would change if we thought of Him more as a romantic interest than a parent. That thought alone would change the entire dynamic of our relationship with God. Sin wouldn't just be considered "something bad we shouldn't do", but rather as cheating and a betrayal against the one we love most.

Thinking in romantic terms suddenly makes Him more accessible, more personal, more present, more reachable, more touchable, more understandable and more *real* even.

Why don't we start letting God fill the void of the Love role we are missing in our lives? If we are missing the Love of a parent, sibling, spouse, or friend, why not let and Love God in a way that fills that void in our lives? Why don't we let God's Love fill in the missing parts of us so that we can be complete?

While our spirits are limited by our human bodies and human minds, we must start finding ways of thinking, and using our entire "human" box of thinking to get as close to God as possible. I know everyone always says the best thing that you can do is think outside of the box, but I think when it comes to Love and relationships it is a good idea to explore every corner of that box before trying to step out of it. And in this case our "box" is our humanity.

I believe that as Christians and believers of God, that we should start exploring every facet of our relationship with God to see which one brings us closer to Him. And once we find the relationship that works best for us, we should never let go of it, no matter what anyone says. Faith is all about getting closer to the truth in what it is that you believe.

John 14:19-21

New International Version (NIV)

19 Before long, the world will not see me anymore, but you will see me. Because I live, you also will live. 20 On that day you will realize that I am in my Father, and you are in me, and I am in you. 21 Whoever has my commands and keeps them is the one who loves me. The one who loves me will be loved by my Father, and I too will love them and show myself to them."

John 14:23-24

New International Version (NIV)

23 Jesus replied, "Anyone who loves me will obey my teaching. My Father will love them, and we will come to them and make our home with them. 24 Anyone who does not love me will not obey my teaching. These words you hear are not my own; they belong to the Father who sent me.

WHEN FAITH IS ITS OWN REWARD

Have you ever heard the saying, "Knowledge is Power?" The reason why we believe that knowledge so powerful is because it is one of the few things which we possess that cannot be taken away. I've noticed recently that Faith is the same way.

When we look at the story of Job, God allowed Job to lose all that he possessed. As we read into the story further, we see that he loses his livestock (his source of wealth and income), his home, his children, and even his health. Although God allowed the devil to take all Job possessed, and even when he lay dying on his sick bed; there was one thing which the devil couldn't take: His Faith!

It is a curious thing to lose everything you've worked for; even some of the things which you have believed for. When we lose these things, we experience grief.

According to famed psychiatrist Elisabeth Kübler-Ross, grief has 5 stages: Denial, Anger, Bargaining, Depression and Acceptance. When grieving, first we are in denial about the loss, then we are angry about the loss, next we try to bargain against the loss, then we enter a depression due to this loss, before we can finally accept the loss.

In our grief over these things we have lost, we go through our brains trying to find solutions to our problems. We question God, pray to God, become angry with God when he doesn't answer and then…we become silent. Our silence is like our personal way of punishing God for the way in which we believe He has punished us. But, after a short (or sometimes long) period of silence, the Christian in us kicks in, and we can't continue to ignore our savior.

The silence makes us lonely, and the depression leaves us with no other option but to hope again; to believe again. Even when we have lost what is most precious to us, but can still feel that spark of Faith, that is its own reward. When our world is crumbling down around us, our Faith in God is like a slap to the devil's face. Satan may be able to divest us of some of our worldly possessions (as he did with Job), but he can't touch our special strength; our spiritual Faith.

"This" Faith makes us feel strong. Even in our times of inner darkness, "this" Faith is the last little bit of light that refuses to fade out, letting us know that soon it will all be okay. And sometimes believing and *knowing* it's all going to be okay, is a type of medicine to the soul.

The message which I'm trying to convey is that the **obtaining** of the things we have Faith for is not the reward, but that **Faith** itself is. It reminds us that while our current state of being (whether we are penniless, lonely, depressed, distraught, or barely hanging on) may make us feel powerless, that last shred of Faith which we possess is strength that can never be taken away from us. We are strong, and through "this" feeling of Faith we are rewarded. It gives us the strength to laugh at the devil when it seems he is laughing at us. It gives us the strength to tell the devil that he has no power here in our lives, in our bodies, in our relationships, or in our minds.

"This" type of Faith on its own, is its own reward.

<u>Job 1:20-22</u>

Amplified Bible (AMP)

[20] Then Job arose and rent his robe and shaved his head and fell down upon the ground and worshiped

[21] And said, Naked (without possessions) came I [into this world] from my mother's womb, and naked (without possessions) shall I depart. The Lord gave and the Lord has taken away; blessed (praised and magnified in worship) be the name of the Lord!

[22] In all this Job sinned not nor charged God foolishly.

NEVER LEAVE YOU
NOR FORSAKE YOU

I will never leave you nor forsake you is what God promises us in the bible; but have we ever taken the time to promise the same to God? Do we not make this promise because we are scared that we can't keep it, or is there something "out there" that we love more than God that prevents us from making this promise?

I believe that if we truly fall in love with God, making this promise will not seem like some impossible task, rather it becomes a natural part of our living. This promise becomes something to feel proud of that empowers us. I believe that if we can make the same promise to God that He has made to us, we would be invincible in our belief. We would form more of a partnership with God rather than just being a servant trying their hardest to be subservient to a master that they feel they can never please, or whose expectations they feel they could never live up to. When we decide deep down inside ourselves that we will never leave or forsake God, a bond is formed and sealed; then nothing, absolutely nothing will be able to separate us from the Love of God.

Hebrews 13:5

New International Version (NIV)

5 Keep your lives free from the love of money and be content with what you have, because God has said, "Never will I leave you; never will I forsake you."

Deuteronomy 31:6

New King James Version (NKJV)

6 Be strong and of good courage, do not fear nor be afraid of them; for the Lord your God, He is the One who goes with you. He will not leave you nor forsake you."

Romans 8:31-39

New Living Translation (NLT)

Nothing Can Separate Us from God's Love

31 What shall we say about such wonderful things as these? If God is for us, who can ever be against us? 32 Since he did not spare even his own Son but gave him up for us all, won't he also give us everything else? 33 Who dares accuse us whom God has chosen for his own? No one—for God himself has given us right standing with himself. 34 Who then will condemn us? No one—for Christ Jesus died for us and was raised to life for us, and he is sitting in the place of honor at God's right hand, pleading for us.

35 Can anything ever separate us from Christ's love? Does it mean he no longer loves us if we have trouble or calamity, or are persecuted, or hungry, or destitute, or in danger, or threatened with death? 36 (As the Scriptures say, "For your sake we are killed every day; we are being slaughtered like sheep.") 37 No, despite all these things, overwhelming victory is ours through Christ, who loved us.

38 And I am convinced that nothing can ever separate us from God's love. Neither death nor life, neither angels nor demons, neither our fears for today nor our worries about tomorrow —not even the powers of hell can separate us from God's love. 39 No power in the sky above or in the earth below— indeed, nothing in all creation will ever be able to separate us from the love of God that is revealed in Christ Jesus our Lord.

Psalm 63:2-4

New International Version (NIV)

2 I have seen you in the sanctuary and beheld your power and your glory. 3 Because your love is better than life, my lips will glorify you. 4 I will praise you as long as I live, and in your name I will lift up my hands.

John 10:17-18

New Life Version (NLV)

17 "For this reason My Father loves Me. It is because I give My life that I might take it back again. 18 No one takes my life from Me. I give it by Myself. I have the right and the power to take it back again. My Father has given Me this right and power."

ALL FOR ONE, AND
ONE FOR ALL

All for one and one for all was the Musketeers' Cree. It makes me wonder if Alexander Dumas wasn't a deeply spiritual man after all. Isn't that what Christ was all about? All for one and one for all? All of us as God's children are one, and Christ as one, delivered us all.

I've heard it said that the belief that we are different from one another is just a trick that our mind plays on us. In reality we aren't different, we are the same. I believe that this is evident in fact that we hurt when we see others hurt, we *feel* filled with love and joy when we observe love and joy being lathered onto those around us. We "*feel*" each other's feelings and emotions, even though we view others as "*others*"; as strange to us and different from ourselves. This is evident when someone in the room is angry or upset about something, and it starts to make everyone else *feel* uncomfortable.

Being told we are different from each other is the lie; it is the untruth whispered to us by a people and a society who have yet to understand the truth. *The truth is that we are one.* I believe the reason that God commanded us to love our neighbor as ourselves, is because our neighbor is "*our self*". We are one and the same. By loving our neighbors, we demonstrate love not only to them, but to ourselves and God as well; thereby completing a never-ending circle of love and "oneness" between our neighbors (others), ourselves, and our God.

<u>1 Corinthians 12:12-13</u>

New Living Translation (NLT)

12 The human body has many parts, but the many parts make up one whole body. So it is with the body of Christ. 13 Some of us are Jews, some are Gentiles, some are slaves, and some are free. But we have all been baptized into one body by one Spirit, and we all share the same Spirit.

Mark 12:31

New Living Translation (NLT)

31 The second is equally important: 'Love your neighbor as yourself. No other commandment is greater than these."

1 John 2:2

New Living Translation (NLT)

2 He himself is the sacrifice that atones for our sins— and not only our sins but the sins of all the world.

2 Corinthians 5:21

New Living Translation (NLT)

21 For God made Christ, who never sinned, to be the offering for our sins, so that we could be made right with God through Christ.

All for one and one for all!

HEAVEN OR HELL? ARE THESE MY ONLY OPTIONS?

Once upon a time, in a land close to yours, there was a
girl and her father:

One day the father asked the girl, "If there were
no heaven, would you still serve God?"

Being of a young age and a malleable mind, this question stuck
with me. As a Christian you are taught to love God, serve God,
follow the rules, and if you do this right, heaven is your reward.
So, the real question is: If there were no rewards for serving
God, would you still serve Him? Please, answer honestly. Upon
being asked this question by my father, I started to think
about my answer. If I answered no, then this would make me
a *shallow* but textbook Christian. But, if I answered yes, then
what? Does answering yes mean my love for God is pure? And by
answering yes, does this in essence make me a non-Christian?

This one question asked of me during my formative years really
changed the way I perceived my relationship with God, and
how I viewed myself as a Christian. And so, from this point on,
I endeavored to be the "Christian" who could answer yes to this
question. I don't know if this endeavor has been good or bad?
On one hand, I am the type of "Christian" who can answer
yes to this question. I can honestly say that I serve and love
God just for being God, not because He's got a Golden Mansion
in the sky "with my name on it". If I can just hear the words
from God's mouth," *You have done well, my good and faithful
servant*", then I'm good. I don't need a heaven after that. Those
words from God's mouth directed at me, that's heaven.

So now that I've conditioned heaven out of my
Christian mind, what do I think about the afterlife?
Can I be real? If so, here it is: I don't want one.

One life is hard enough, and I don't want another one, even if it is in the sky! If I could choose a reward to be given to me from God for a good Christian life lived with Him, it would be only this: A good life and a peaceful death. Upon my death I would like to hear the words I stated earlier and then happily to fall into the oblivion of non-existence.

This is why I ask if my pursuit of a yes answer to my father's question is good or bad. When presented with the prospect of heaven or hell, I choose neither. I'm "in love" with God. I'm in love with God and serve him not only for all of the wonderful blessings that He has chosen to give to me thus far in my life, but I'm also in love with and serve Him for the mere fact that He exists; that he always has and always will. I'm in love with and serve Him for being my first friend, and my constant life companion. I'm in love with and serve Him for listening to me when I pray, during my episodes of depression and when I rant and rave. I am just in love with Him because He's there, because he lives, and because even though sometimes I may resent it, he chose me to attach himself to. And really and truly this is enough,

...Sometimes